To all the

Joe Mac

Jesuit Geometers

A Study of Fifty-six Prominent Jesuit Geometers During the First Two Centuries of Jesuit History

by

Joseph MacDonnell, S.J.
Professor of Mathematics
Fairfield University

ἀγεωμέτρητος μηδεὶς εἰσίτω μου τὴν στέγην

Let no one unversed in geometry enter my door

Plato's Academy

St. Louis
Institute of Jesuit Sources

Vatican City
Vatican Observatory Publications

First Edition

Published jointly by:
The Institute of Jesuit Sources
and
The Vatican Observatory

Number 11 in Series IV of the Institute of Jesuit Sources:
Studies in Jesuit Topics

Distributed (except in Italy and Vatican City State) by:

The Institute of Jesuit Sources
St. Louis University
3700 West Pine Blvd.
St. Louis, Missouri 63108

Distributed in Italy and Vatican City State by:

Libreria Editrice Vaticana
V-00120 Citta' del Vaticano
Vatican City State

Library of Congress Catalog Card number: 89-80568

ISBN 0-912422-94-7

Dedication

I dedicate this book to the Clavius Group, composed of Jesuit mathematicians and their colleagues - that merry band of scholars who continually astonish other professional mathematicians because they actually help and inspire one another.

Joseph MacDonnell, S.J.

Guldin

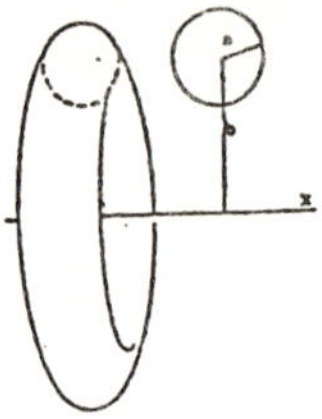

Lana-Terzi

Riccati

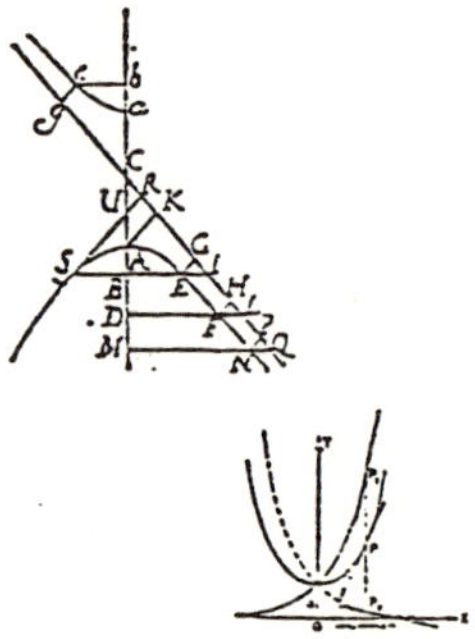

Some

Jesuit Geometers

and their

Geometry

d'Aguilon

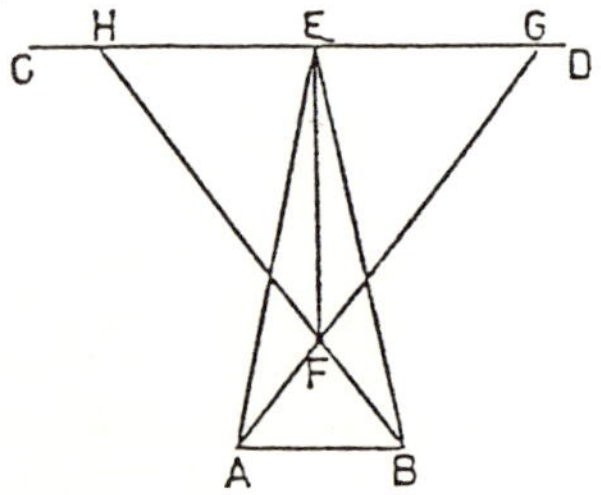

Scheiner

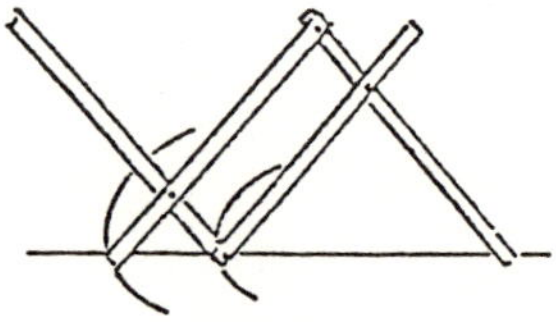

Pozzo

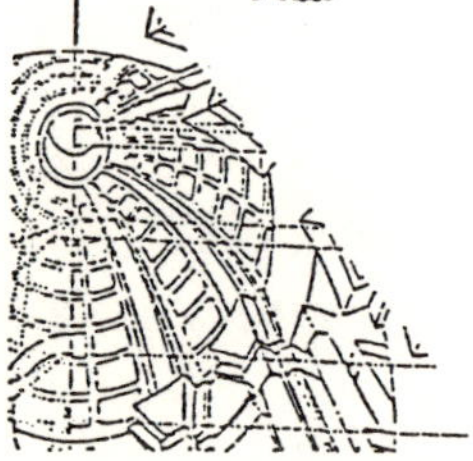

Sarasa

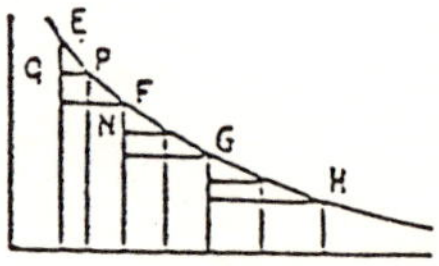

by

Joseph MacDonnell, S.J.

Boscovich

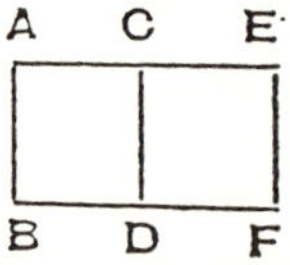

Forward

This study, *Jesuit Geometers*, published in cooperation with the Vatican Observatory, marks for the Institute of Jesuit Sources both a distinctive and a happy addition to its list of titles.

First of all, it is distinctive in being the first joint publication of the two institutions. It is further distinctive in that, whereas the Vatican Observatory has a long and distinguished record for the variety and quality of its publications in the physical and mathematical sciences, this is the first book from the Institute of Jesuit Sources to deal with a subject in those fields.

The Institute published its first book in 1964. Over the twenty-five intervening years, some three dozen books in several series have appeared, each in its own way aimed at fulfilling the Institute's overall purpose, that of making the sources of Jesuit thought and activity more readily available to readers in the English-speaking world. To this end, the Institute provides English translations both of Jesuit primary sources and of modern foreign-language studies about the Jesuits, and also publishes scholarly studies and other works of a larger and more general interest about the Jesuits originally written in English. The present volume belongs to the last-named series.

For a long time the Institute has wanted to include among its offerings a work that dealt with Jesuits in the sciences. Until now its books have revolved around areas where Jesuit life and activity have intersected with history, theology, the social sciences, education, and biblical scholarship. The present book broadens the scope of the Institute's publications to the fields of mathematics, especially geometry, and the physical sciences and to special disciplines such as astronomy and architecture.

Jesuit Geometers is not only a distinctive addition to our list; it is also a happy one. This engagingly-written study draws together from a great variety of disparate and scattered resources information not otherwise easily available on the lives and thought and activity of a group of men who over the space of two centuries contributed to the progress of geometry and to the disciplines related to it. Differing in time, nationality, temperament, and specialization, these geometers were similar in that they were all members of the Society of Jesus which was an influential factor in the world of science during the first two centuries of its existence. To recall to memory in this book these men and their distinguished contributions is a happy circumstance. Just as important and pleasant is the opportunity through this study to recognize with gratitude the multifarious ways in which secular scientists, working with members of the Society of Jesus over the centuries in the common endeavor of scientific research and teaching, have by their insights and examples enriched the lives and work of countless Jesuits. Lastly, this book furnishes an occasion to honor all those Jesuits who, pursuing the sciences with the rigor and honesty that they demand, have testified to the intrinsic importance and value of scientific knowledge on its own terms and at the same time have been responsive to the call of Ignatius Loyola, the founder of the Jesuits, to "seek and find God in all things."

John W. Padberg, S.J.

Director and General Editor
The Institute of Jesuit Sources.

Table of Contents

Index of Illustrations

Page

Chapter 1

Chapter 2

Chapter 3

Preface

For the first two centuries of Jesuit history 631 Jesuit geometers are listed in Sommervogel's twelve volume work *Bibliotheque de la Compagnie de Jesus*[1] where their publications are evaluated and described. The title *Jesuit Geometers,* however, might seem incongruous since the word *Jesuit* conjures up images of martyrs and missionaries like Brebeuf, Xavier and deNobile, theologians like Suarez, the Church Militant exemplified in Bellarmine, or preachers like Bourdaloue. On the other hand Euclid, Appolonius, Menelaus, Descartes, Fermat, Euler, Desargues and Lobachevski were geometers but not Jesuits. So what does the Society of Jesus have to do with geometry? In the educational work of the Society geometry played a very important role right from the very beginning. Apart from their classroom teaching, many Jesuits by their curiosity, ingenuity, correspondence, and publications contributed greatly to the growth of geometry. Their practical geometrical inventions, their discoveries of new forms of geometry, and their innovations in the teaching of geometry contributed greatly to its development. Furthermore their knowledge of geometry proved an invaluable aid in establishing missions in all parts of the world so that non-Jesuit, non-Catholic, non-Christian geometers benefited from their labors and skill. While there is no such thing as Jesuit geometry, it is certain that the geometries so familiar today would have a different form and encompass far less if these men had never existed.

During their first two centuries the Jesuits were involved in an explosion of intellectual activity, engaged in over 700 schools. Then suddenly these were all lost in 1773. During the 1769 conclave the Franciscan Friar Lorenzo Ganganelli became Pope Clement XIV. Four years later, yielding to pressure from the Bourbon courts, fearing the loss of his Papal States, and anticipating that other European countries would follow the example of Henry VIII, he issued his brief *Dominus ac Redemptor* suppressing the Society. This religious order of twenty-three thousand men dedicated to the service of the church was disbanded. All seminarians were sent home, all houses given away, and the Jesuit general Lorenzo Ricci was arrested and put in solitary confinement in the prison of Castel Sant' Angelo, where he died a few years later. The property of the Society's many schools was either sold or made over into a state controlled system. The Society's libraries were broken up and the books either burned, sold or snatched up by those who collaborated in the suppression. Ever since then the Society's books have been appearing in private collections of book harvesters or in the great libraries throughout the world. The unusual method of promulgation of the brief of suppression (wherein each bishop had to proclaim it to all Jesuits within his jurisdiction) caused perplexing canonical difficulties. So when Catherine, Empress of Russia, rejected the brief outright and forbade its promulgation, 200 Jesuits continued to function in Russia. The Society was restored 41 years later in 1814 by Pope Pius VII, who celebrated the feast of St Ignatius by reading the bull *Sollicitudo Omnium Ecclesiarum* , revoking the suppression, in the presence of 150 members of the suppressed society. Although many of the men had died by then, the memory of their educational enterprise had not, and the new Society was flooded with requests to take over colleges: in France alone, for instance, 86 schools were offered to the Jesuits; of course they could accept only a few.

The Jesuits have had more than their share of enemies but even the bitterest would not deny their mathematical accomplishments. These have, however, been minimized by past historians. The claim, for instance, was made that Jesuits were Aristotelians and therefore were not open to modern geometrical trends or that their religious convictions hindered free inquiry. The assumption was that only agnostics are truly free from bias and able to pursue truth with an open mind. An earlier edition of the Encyclopedia Britannica (the eleventh) branded the work of Jesuit geometers as "respectable mediocrity". Later editions leave out this derogatory passage, which is not shared by modern historians. Another problem occurs when some writers unskilled in church matters, make the assumption that all priests are Jesuits. Thus an article in *Scientific American*[2] blames the suicide of Galois' father on the "Jesuit priest of Bourg-la-Reine". Although this occurred at a time when there were no Jesuits within hundreds of miles. And, finally, some Jesuit mathematicians and scientists have not been identified as Jesuits.[3] The world famous Jesuit astronomer Angelo Secchi, S.J. of the past century has been referred to as P. (for Pater) Secchi. The P. Secchi has been transformed into Pietro Secchi by an inventive writer.[4]

The purpose of this work is to examine these Jesuit geometers and their accomplishments during the 17th and 18th centuries while geometry was in a crucial stage of its development. Their effective influence on the growth of geometry should be evident from their original thinking, inventions, innovations, publications, teaching, correspondence and their determination to disseminate geometrical concepts accurately. Their evaluation by their peers and by later professionals makes it even more evident.

These two centuries between 1570 and 1770 were also critical in the growth of mathematics during the time the calculus was evolving. Discoveries were being made and concepts developed which enabled giants like Newton and Euler to articulate the foundations of modern analysis. In particular it was a critical time for geometry because not only were the seeds being planted for the later geometries but also proofs of the precalculus as well as the calculus principles had to be geometrical. Until the time of Fermat and Descartes nongeometrical proofs simply were not acceptable: Newton, for example, proved his theorems geometrically. The motto of the American Mathematical Society, founded a hundred years ago in 1888, was inspired by Clio, the muse of history, and Urania, the muse of mathematics and astronomy. It reminds its readers that admittance to Plato's academy requires geometry.[5] A rough translation of the Greek inscription is: "Let no one unversed in geometry enter my door."

Furthermore, *geometry* in these centuries came to include not only the synthetic geometry of Euclid but all kinds of applications: dyalling, gnomonics, geometrical optics, map-making, stereometry, plane and spherical trigonometry. The need for rigor and logic was being recognized, also, and it was in geometry that this need was felt most acutely. Histories of geometry may emphasize the works of these aforementioned giants, but the story of geometry cannot be fully appreciated without examining the contributions of the lesser geometers in order to trace how the ideas originated, in order to gain a fuller understanding of the concepts. In his *History of Mathematics* Carl Boyer quotes Newton writing to Hooke: "If I have seen farther than Descartes, it is because I have stood on the shoulders of giants."[6]

On the other hand, the same two centuries were critical for Jesuits since the young society grew from ten members in 1540 to twenty-three thousand members at the time of the suppression in 1773. The number of Jesuit schools in Europe kept increasing so that it became the largest school system in Europe. Around the middle of the eighteenth century, the Jesuits operated 740 educational institutions throughout the world 14 of which were universities. Besides this, Jesuits taught in 11 state universities. In particular it was a critical time for Jesuit geometers since they were engaged in the great creative innovations in geometry. George Sarton spoke of the Jesuit mathematicians of the time in his article *An Appeal for the Republication in Book Form of Fr. Bosmans' Studies* [7]. "One cannot talk about mathematics in the 16th and 17th centuries without seeing a Jesuit at every corner".

The story of the Jesuit contribution to geometry at this time has not been told, even though much work has been done by Jesuit historians such as Henri Bosmans. Conor Reilly noted that "Jesuits have done little to reveal the contributions of their predecessors to the foundations of modern science."[8] Jesuits, furthermore, are challenged by the historian D. J. Struik: "When are you Jesuits going to write a coherent history of Jesuit mathematics based on the groundwork of Henri Bosmans?"[9]

This work is certainly not an adequate response to Struik's invitation but may serve as a step in that direction. It is not meant to be a history of Jesuit mathematics but rather a story about Jesuit mathematicians; it does not describe the details of their geometry but instead stresses the contributions Jesuits made during the development of geometry. All of the 56 men mentioned wrote books on geometry. They were, therefore, geometers, even though many of them worked in other fields as well. Indeed, some were better known as astronomers, physicists or "philosophers of nature." These men were not of the stature of Newton and Euler but were some of the lesser geometers mentioned above whose story should be told. To speak only of Jesuit geometers here does not mean that other geometers were doing nothing; on the contrary a common effort and exchange of ideas occurred that moved geometry forward and made it possible for the greater mathematicians to discover and articulate the major breakthroughs leading to the calculus. The story of similar non-Jesuit geometers can be told elsewhere.

The exchange of ideas was not only through letters and publications but also through the normal teacher/student process. After a teacher presented his analysis, an alert student would take the notes and try to improve on the matter and then later as a teacher pass the improved version on to the next group of students. Jesuits and non-Jesuits quoted each other without always giving credit. Euclid, for instance, was not accused of this, yet he was writing down what was the accumulated geometrical wisdom of that time. Galileo made very free use of Jesuit geometers' teaching notes without making any acknowledgment.[10] While serious priority arguments did occur, historians have, perhaps, made accusations of plagiarism too lightly without considering the spirit of the times.

A case in point is that of the Jesuit **Paul Guldin**, author of **Guldin's** rule for finding volumes of revolution by using the center of gravity. A few decades ago some authors and publishers had removed his name from calculus textbooks and substituted Pappus' name because an unfounded accusation of plagiarism was believed. It has been well established by modern historians, specialists in that era, such as Paul Ver Eecke, that **Guldin** was falsely accused. The *Dictionary of*

Scientific Biography (DSB) brings up another problem regarding false accusations about Jesuit scientists and the fact that after the suppression of the Jesuits in 1773 they had no forum to defend themselves. Konradin D'Occhieppo speaks of "the public defamation of the Jesuits then in vogue."[11] The case regards **Maximilian Hell**, the Jesuit geometer-astronomer accused of falsifying his data. He was not cleared of this calumny for over a century.

One word of caution about these centuries. It would be a mistake to assume that ease in transportation and communication were in any sense analogous to that of today, and to forget that books and publications were not immediately available. Discussion and seminars were sometimes impossible. In fact travel was often impossible because wars were continuous and the English anti-Jesuit laws were in force with a vengeance. Jesuit communities and schools, like others, did not escape these perils and the turmoil of the times. It was a time when a whole community, caught between warring factions, would be suddenly set upon and massacred. In 1594 for instance the Jesuits were forced out of the College de la Trinité following an attempt on the life of Henry IV by one of their students. One member of the community was hanged, another stretched on the rack and the student was torn apart by horses. In 1582, the fourth day of October was followed by the fifteenth day of October and 10 days were dropped when Clavius' calender was adopted. This precipitated riots, as well as rocks hurled at the windows of Jesuit houses by irate citizens whose lives suddenly became complicated. In the past some historians seem to have forgotten the turmoil of the times when making judgments about irregularities occurring in Jesuit contributions to geometry and science.

The real contribution of Jesuit geometers can best be understood from the numerous Jesuit specialists in geometry, and so in Appendix 2 is found a list of 105 Jesuit geometers who are listed in Sommervogel's *Bibliothèque de la Compagnie de Jésus*. There are 470 more, not listed. Also there is a shorter list in Appendix 1 of the 56 more prominent Jesuit geometers, describing their lives and their contributions. These latter **56 Jesuit Geometers** appear in **bold print** in the text. The main body of this work concerns the contributions these men made in the growth of geometrical studies. Books by Eves, Boyer, Struik, the encyclopedias and the Dictionary of Scientific Biography all have impressive descriptions of them and their work. Less available, but more to the point are the many writings of Henri Bosmans,[12] a Jesuit mathematician and mathematics historian of a later century. The library of the house of writers in Rome, *Institutum Historicum Societatis Jesu* (IHSJ), has a rich collection of these and similar articles about Jesuit geometers.

In this work I draw on all these sources especially the non-Jesuit sources such as the *Dictionary of Scientific Biography* (DSB) and *The Philosophical Transactions of the Royal Society* (TRS). I also wish to express my gratitude to patient proof readers, John L. McCarthy, Martin McCarthy, Frank Lewis and Joan Hanlon, not to mention the genius of Frederick Kelly who computed my index and Charles Johnson who did many of the sketches.

I attempted to keep the illustrations consistent, so they are mostly sketches (some my own) of whatever pictures were available of these men and their works. It must be remembered that Kodak appeared on the scene centuries later. While attempting to steer a course between the callous neglect of the Jesuit effort, and inordinate triumphalism, I try to make the case that geometers of today owe much to the Jesuit geometers of the 17th and 18th centuries. The evidence for this Jesuit influence is divided into six parts:

1. their textbooks and publications
2. their inventions in practical geometry
3. their innovations in the various fields of geometry
4. the indirect influence they have had through teaching and correspondence
5. their teaching innovations, methods and attitudes
6. the evaluation of these geometers by professionals, then and now

This same argument comes by way of reluctant testimony from Francis Bacon, scarcely a Jesuit enthusiast, in his work *The Advancement of Learning*. He was commenting on the Jesuits' influence on science.

> This excellent part of ancient discipline, has in some measure been revived of late by the colleges of Jesuits abroad. . . . And of late years the Jesuits, partly of themselves and partly provoked by example, have greatly enlivened and strengthened the state of learning.[13]

Preface Footnotes

1. Carolus Sommervogel: Bruxelles: Societe Belge de Libraire, 1890-1960.
2. *Scientific American.* April, 1982, p. 141.
3. Morris Kline: *Mathematical thought from ancient to modern times.* New York: 1972. Examples can be found in this history by Morris Kline. Without mentioning the fact that Gregory St. Vincent is a Jesuit, he credits him with setting the groundwork for analytic geometry (p. 356), with discovering the connection between the hyperbola and the logarithm function (p. 354) and of contributing important transformations to the study of projective geometry (p. 300). In a similar manner he deals with the Jesuit geometers Claude F.M. de Chales and Paul Guldin.
   Some of the best known textbook sketches such as Schott's Magdeburg experiment (p. 47) and Kircher's Tower of Babel (p. 73) are used without credit to these Jesuits. Archimedes' Burning Mirror taken from Kircher's Ars Magna, is found in the 1985 book *Mathematics and optimal form* by S. Hildebrand and A. Tromba on page 53 with no mention of Kircher.
4. *Astronomy Today.* Milwaukee: May, vol. 15 #5, 1987, p. 36.
5. Plato's academy was a grotto; the door is metaphorical. The A. M. S. motto is an abbreviation of Plato's original.
6. Carl Boyer: *History of Mathematics.* 1968, p. 429.
7. *ISIS: International Review devoted to the history of science and civilization.* Bruges: St. Catherine Press, vol. 40, 1949, p. 3-6.
8. *Bulletin of the American Association of Jesuit Scientists.* vol 42, 1965, p. 12-15. Besides these Jesuits, Bosmans and Reilly, I am also indebted to the historical works of the Jesuit authors Thomas Mulchrone, Edward Phillips and Frederick Homann.
9. *Ibid.,* vol 34, 1957 p. 53.
10. William Wallace, O.P.: *Galileo's early notebooks.* Notre Dame: Notre Dame Press, 1977. One of the principal points of Wallace is that Galileo received many of his ideas concerning the motion of heavenly bodies from the Jesuits teaching at the Roman College.
11. DSB vol. 6, p. 234.
12. A. Rome: "Le R.P. Henri Bosmans" in ISIS vol. 12, 1929, p. 88-112.
13. Francis Bacon:*The Advancement of Learning.* ed. by Joseph Devey, NewYork: 1902 p. 50,71.

Chapter 1 Publications in Geometry

During the centuries preceding and during the discovery of calculus, the numerous geometry books written by Jesuits were widely used in the colleges throughout Europe. Most books were in Latin with elaborate dedications to the current potentates. Many were written on rather substantial paper (though not wormproof) and as a result have lasted through the centuries. The careful record of Jesuit publications during this period is available in the 12-volume work of Sommervogel, which lists and evaluates more than 18,000 publications. This massive work describes the books written by Jesuits since the very beginning of the Jesuit Society, and it is most accurate for the earlier centuries. The tenth volume lists the Jesuit geometers of the 17th and 18th centuries so that the number of authors can be counted and classified according to 13 subdivisions of geometry (for example, there are 77 authors of ordinary Euclidean geometry). Sommervogel lists the number of authors in each subdivision as follows:[1]

77	Euclidean geometry
15	the art of measuring
13	analytic geometry
48	the sphere
54	trigonometry
12	logarithms
26	navigation
80	gnomonics and horology
44	the calendar
74	military fortifications
22	geometry applied to calculus
49	geometry applied to astronomy
117	geometry applied to mechanics

CHRISTOPHORI
CLAVII BAMBER-
GENSIS E SOCIETATE
IESV.

GEOMETRIA
PRACTICA.

1 Title page of *Geometrica Practica* by Christopher Clavius (called the "Euclid of the sixteenth century") reprinted many times, even after the suppression of the Jesuit Society.

Some of these 631 authors have written only one geometry book, but some have written many more. **Athanasius Kircher** for example wrote 39 books, **Roger Boscovich** 151, of which Sommervogel lists only 103. Many of the books described in Sommervogel have gone to multiple editions. **André Tacquet's** geometry as well as **Christopher Clavius**' books were used for centuries in the European schools. Some of these books have been reprinted in this century and are available today. Not all books, of course, were of equal value and some became obsolete in a few years as geometry rapidly grew and the geometrical emphasis changed. But one thing is clear: the Jesuits realized how important would be the printed word for the development of geometry.

Today these books are found in rare book collections such as Yale's *Beinecke*

Library, Berkeley's *Bancroft* Library and Kansas City's *Linda Hall* Library of science and technology. A large number are found in the libraries of the Jesuit Curia as well as the Jesuit House of Writers in Rome. Some books have not survived, perhaps because of overly tidy Jesuit housekeepers who tend to throw out any publication more than a month old. One book that seems to have survived very well is the very difficult book of **Clavius** *In sphaeram Joannis de Sacrobosco* (Rome 1581). It is a commentary on the widely used thirteenth- century book concerning the geometry of the sphere and its astronomical implications, written by John Halifax (also called Hollywood, or in Latin, "Sacrobosco"). **Clavius'** commentary, although in very small print, on crowded pages, with notes jammed into the margins, is called the best commentary on *Sacrobosco* ever done. Another book, **Clavius'** *Euclid* also has survived perhaps because it was reprinted so often and was so widely used: it was the text used throughout Europe for some time - used by Descartes and Mersenne at La Flèche for instance. This book was not merely Euclid's elements of geometry but a careful commentary. It contained many original theorems as well as some axioms Euclid missed, for example an axiom concerning proportion. Also, **Clavius** showed that he appreciated Euclid's wisdom in adding the famous fifth postulate. In acknowledgement of his mastery of all geometry, **Clavius** was given the title "Euclid of the l6th Century." As he wrote in a letter to Jean Bernoulli, Leibniz was led to an interest in mathematics by reading books by Jesuits such as **Clavius** and **Gregory St. Vincent**[2]. The mathematical historian Moritz Cantor speaks of the influence of **Clavius'** books and why they went into so many editions.

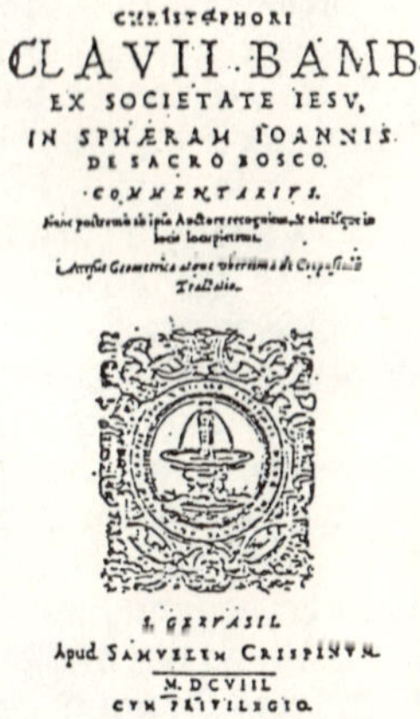

2 Title page of Clavius' *In Sphaeram Joannis de Sacrobosco* "The best commentary on the *Sphere* ever written".

> The large number of editions which were needed to satisfy the demand for his *Euclid* shows the high reputation which the work achieved. Seldom has so high a reputation been so well earned . . . Clavius shows an acute critical faculty. He detected and exposed old errors. There is no difficulty that he attempted to evade. . . . This work of Clavius is indispensable even today for historical research.[3]

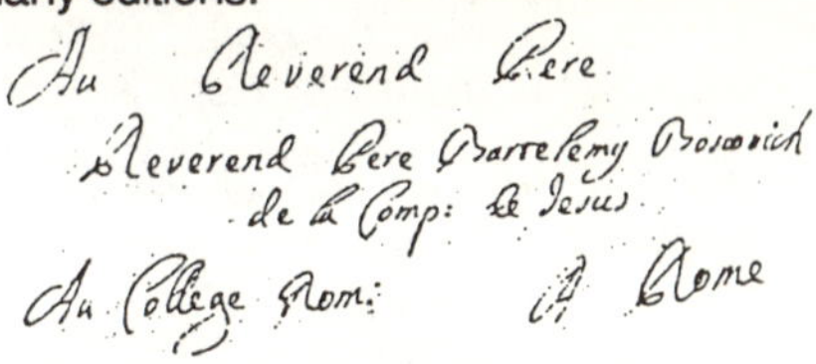
3 Address of one of several hundred letters Roger Boscovich wrote to his Jesuit brother Bartholomew Boscovich: now found in the Boscovich collection in the Bancroft library of rare books at The University of California at Berkeley.

Another historian Abraham Kaestner refers to **Clavius'** *Geometrica Practica* (1604) as "a model textbook of practical geometry, perfect for its time." **Clavius** is even better remembered for his work in astronomy and has been referred to as the "best-selling scientific author of the Renaissance."

A book by **Gregory St. Vincent** included in the title the unfortunate words "Quadratura Circuli". In it he erroneously claimed to have squared the circle; i.e. formed a square x^2 equal in area to a given circle radius R so $\mathbf{x^2 = \pi R^2}$. This would mean of course that π is an algebraic number (the root of a polynomial equation with rational coefficients). The fact that π is transcendental and not algebraic was not proven until a century later. Many mathematicians who became known as "circle squarers," spent their energies trying to solve this futile problem, just as mathematicians tried to prove Fermat's last theorem in a later time. The Royal Society of London had to issue a plea: "Please send no more articles on squaring the circle". Like Fermat's last theorem, however, a great deal of mathematics was learned in the effort. **St. Vincent's** book was mostly concerned with other forms of geometry such as the study of infinitesimals and coordinates, which was quite valuable, and earned him the honor of being one of the founders of analytic geometry.[4] Only the last chapter of his book dealt with squaring the circle, but it was enough to hold his whole work up to ridicule from later commentators arguing from the safety of hindsight that the problem is unsolvable.

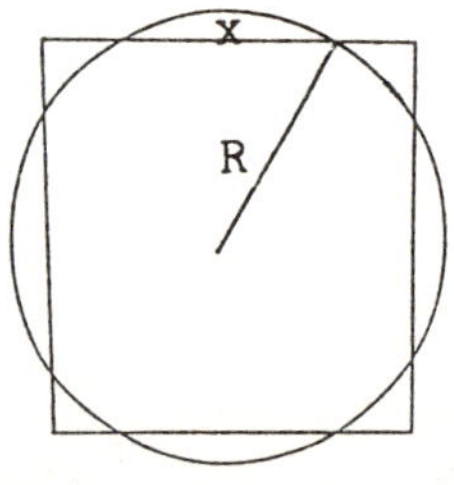

4 Squaring the circle: Find x so that $x^2 = \pi R^2$ The problem which led the *Transactions* to plead: "please send no more proofs!"

Montucla wrote of **St. Vincent**, "No one ever squared the circle with so much ability or so much success (except for the principal object)"[5]. When **St. Vincent** requested permission to publish from his superior general Mutius Vitelleschi, S.J., the latter passed the problem on to **Clavius'** successor **Grienberger**, who spent a year of deliberation with **St. Vincent**. **Grienberger** threw up his hands in despair. "If only **Clavius** were alive now! How I miss his counsel". He was not satisfied with **St. Vincent's** work but in his very enigmatic answer to Vitelleschi he seemed to agree reluctantly, so **Gregory St. Vincent** published the offending chapter on squaring the circle. His response is found in the unedited letters of **Grienberger** published by Henri Bosmans.

> This is my opinion: that Father Gregory should not only *not* be dismissed (from his obligation), but should be constrained until he has left the quadrature in a state where it can no longer be a problem.[6]

Later **St. Vincent** directed the famous school of mathematics at Antwerp founded by **François d'Aguilon** where many Jesuit mathematicians studied. Among the most outstanding of these was **André Tacquet** who published a geometry book *Opera omnia* (Antwerp, 1669) called by Henry Oldenburg, founder of *The Philosophical Transactions of the Royal Society* (TRS), one of the best books ever written about mathematics.[7] It was reviewed in the TRS, giving specific details of the different aspects of geometry dealt with in the book. For instance in the section dealing with indivisibles, Oldenburg reports optimistically on the **Guldin**-Cavalieri dispute: "the controversie, and the reply about it, is exceeding pleasant".[8] Two of **Tacquet's** other works, *Elementa Geometriae* (Anvers, 1654) and *Arithmetica theoria et praxis* (Louvain, 1656) were used as school texts, after being reprinted and translated into Italian and English.

A book by **d'Aguilon** concerns geometrical optics, which in the Jesuit schools was taught under the heading of Geometry. He was given the task of organizing the teaching of geometry and science which would be useful for geography, navigation, architecture and the military arts. His plan was to synthesize the works of former geometers starting with Euclid and apply geometry to the three ways in which the eye perceives: directly, then by reflection and finally by refraction. His death interfered with the publication of the two later sections.

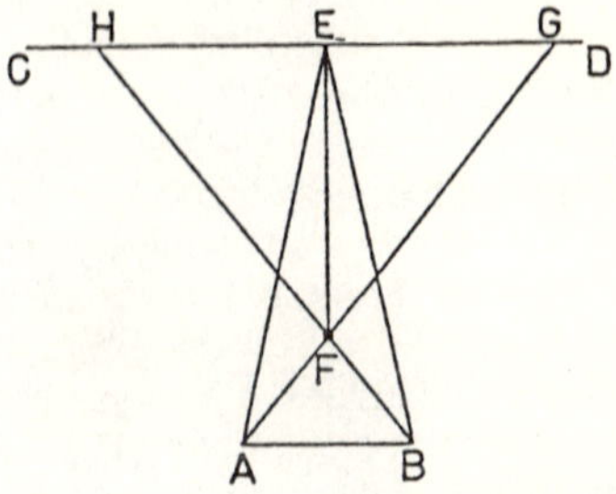

5 Binocular vision discussed by d'Aguilon. Point F is seen by eyes A and B in 3 places G,H or E along the horopter CD depending on whether left, right, or both eyes are open.

His treatment of different kinds of projections, especially stereographic, was meant to aid architects, cosmographers, navigators and artists. The book has a long title *Opticorum libri sex philosophis juxta ac mathematicis utiles* (Anvers, 1613), "Book six of Optics, useful for philosophers and mathematicians alike".

D'Aguilon's book contained a number of original insights and contributions to the field of geometrical optics even though he was unaware of the optical theories established by Kepler's *Optics* several years previously.

It gave some early hints on perspective geometry and was later used by Desargues, the father of projective geometry.[9]

D'Aquilon was the first to use the term horopter, the line drawn through the focal point of both eyes and parallel to the line between the eyes. Binocular vision was not understood at this time: how do two eyes form one integral image since closing one, the other or neither give three different images?

6 One of the Rubens woodcuts for d'Aguilon's *Geometrical Optics*. Found among the mythical figures is the eagle referring to d'Aguilon's name, Mercury holding an Argus' head full of eyes and Minerva with Medusa's head.

Constantijn Huygens read this book at the age of 20, was enthralled by it and later said that is was the best book he had ever read in geometrical optics. He thought that **d'Aguilon** should be compared to Plato, Eudoxus and Archimedes. In fact the title of Constantijn Huygens' first publication imitated **d'Aguilon's** title (omitting letters p and c): *Otiorum Libri Sex* (1625) and his son Christiaan Huygens many years later was still using **d'Aguilon's** book.

What is most remarkable about this book is the fact that the illustrations of each section are works of the greatest Baroque painter of Flanders, Peter Paul Rubens. The frontispiece at the beginning of the book shows an eagle, referring to **d'Aguilon's** name and a variety of optical and geometrical images. On either side of the title stand Mercury holding the head of Argus with a hundred eyes, and Minerva holding a shield reflecting the head of Medusa. Then, at the beginning of each of six sections are Rubens' drawings describing **d'Aguilon's** experiments, one of which is the first known picture of a photometer. This is one of six experiments drawn by Rubens and shows how intensity of light varies with the square of distance from the source. The experiment was later taken up by Mersenne and another Jesuit, **Claude de Chales,** and eventually led to Bouguer's more famous photometer.[10] It is evident, from the detail that he put into his drawings, how enthused Rubens was about the subject matter, perspective geometry and optical rules.

A book written by August Ziggelaar, "*François d'Aguilon, S.J. (1567-1617) Scientist and Architect*" (Rome 1983), concerns the life of **d'Aguilon** and the story of his *Opticorum libri sex* along with the involvement of Rubens. Rubens also designed frontispieces for other Jesuit geometry books, such as the *Theoremata de centro gravitatis* (Antwerp, 1632) of **Jean Charles de la Faille**, a copy of which is kept in the Plantin Museum in Brussels.[11]

7 Roger Boscovich, S.J. (1711-1787) whose bold notion of "point centers" abandoned the old notion of solid atoms. Using geometrical methods and arguments he gave the first coherent description of an atomic theory.

The prize for the largest number of books must go to **Roger Boscovich**, and many of them survive in the **Boscovich** collection in the Bancroft Library of Rare Books at Berkeley (U.C.B.). He published 151 books and treatises, and in his own lifetime a large number of his letters were published as well. The renowned astronomer Joseph de LaLande spoke of these works of **Boscovich**: "In each of these treatises there are ideas worthy of a genius."[12] He first caught de Lalande's attention when, as a young man, he published a geometrical solution to a difficult astronomical problem, and de LaLande liked it so much he included it in his own book.[13]

One of **Boscovich's** major works *Philosophiae naturalis* (Vienna, 1758) in which, among other things, he introduces his **Boscovich** curve of forces,[14] gives the first coherent description of an atomic theory. It was one of the great attempts to understand the structure of the universe in a single idea. He held that bodies could not be composed of continuous matter, but of countless "point-like" structures.

He states that the ultimate elements of matter are indivisible points which are centers of force and this force varies with the distance to other points. This book appeared well over a century before modern atomic theory. The work was often reprinted and was considered so important a contribution to atomic physics that an International Bicentenary Symposium of 1958 was held at Belgrade to commemorate the publication of **Boscovich's** work *Philosophiae naturalis*. Two of the eighteen papers presented were from Niels Bohr and Werner Heisenberg.[15] Another such symposium was held three years later in his home town of Dubrovnik (then Ragusa). Russian scientists have always shown an interest in his work; only recently have Western scientists taken an interest.

Boscovich was primarily a geometer, mainly concerned with the applications of geometrical methods to represent physical phenomena. This is especially noticed in another major work *Elementa universae matheseos* (Rome, 1754) in which is found his treatment of conic sections.[16] **André Tacquet's** very popular *Elementa geometriae* became more popular when a section was added to it containing **Boscovich's** treatise on spherical trigonometry; it was reprinted six times between 1745 and 1780. As often happened with Jesuit geometry books, this book was still used long after the Society of Jesus had been suppressed.[17]

A rather unusual book is the *Repetitio menstrua* (Louvain, 1639) by **Jean Ciermans.** It partitions geometrical sciences according to months of the year. Each of twelve topics - geometry, arithmetic, optics, statics, hydrostatics, nautics, architecture, logic, war-machines, geography, astronomy and chronology is assigned to a given month. The fact that he uses 354 days (a lunar year) instead of 365 and divides the month into three parts as did Moslem writers, indicates that he probably got the idea for this arrangement from some previous Moslem author.

Another example of Jesuit geometrical publications is taken from the middle of the seventeenth century. The historian Morris Kline has high praise for a very popular mathematics book written by **Claude F M de Chales** which applied geometry to all other branches of knowledge. It also had been reviewed in the TRS.

> The compass of mathematics, as understood in the seventeenth century, may be seen from the *Cursus seu Mundus Mathematicus* (The Course or the World of Mathematics) by Claude-François Milliet De Chales (1621-78), published in 1674 and in an enlarged edition in 1690. Aside from arithmetic, trigonometry, and logarithms, he treats practical geometry, mechanics, statics, geography, magnetism, civil engineering, carpentry, stonecutting, military construction, hydrostatics, fluid flow, hydraulics, ship construction, optics, perspective, music, the design of firearms and cannons, the astrolabe, sundials, astronomy, calendar-reckoning, and horoscopy. Finally, he includes algebra, the theory of indivisibles, the theory of conics, and special curves such as the quadratrix and the spiral. This work was popular and esteemed. Though in the inclusion of some topics it reflects Renaissance interests, on the whole it presents a reasonable picture of the seventeenth - and even the eighteenth-century world of mathematics.[18]

Pantometrum Kircherianum (Wurzburg, 1669), a geometrical work describes a geometric calculator invented by the extraordinary Jesuit scientist **Athanasius Kircher**. In the same year he explained a kind of symbolic logic in another book *Ars magna sciendi* (Amsterdam 1669) and in a later book *Tariffa Kircheriana* (Rome, 1679) is a set of mathematical tables. These are three of the 39 books Kircher wrote. Some of them are huge, bigger than altar sacramentaries and with large print as if they were meant to be on continual display. Some of his other books are very well decorated with creative and entertaining drawings, such as his book of the bible stories *Arca Noe* (Amsterdam, 1675). In this book he makes it clear that he understands the evolutionary process; later biologists have been impressed by this remarkably progressive viewpoint.

The other books indicate his widespread interest and genius and why **Kircher** has been compared to Leonardo di Vinci. His first publication concerned magnetism: he emphasized the parallel between the forces of gravity and magnetism. Then he wrote of sundials, next on the Egyptian language, then on calendars, then on the 1656 bubonic plague. In the latter he attributes the plague to tiny animals which he had observed under a microscope. This is one of the earliest hints of what we today call "germs."

8 Athanatius Kircher, S.J. (1602-1680)
"Master of a hundred arts"

In 1680 **Kircher** is said to have correctly computed the ordinary (vs. forced) flight of a swallow at 100 ft/sec - and this before the invention of stopwatches![19]

He wrote about the Coptic language and showed that it was a vestige of early Egyptian. His interest in interpreting the obelisks led him to such a thorough study of the subject that princes, popes and cardinals appointed him to decipher various obelisks. It was not until the discovery of the Rosetta stone in 1799 that anyone else had any success. In fact it was because of **Kircher's** work that scientists knew what to look for when interpreting the Rosetta stone. He has been called the real founder of Egyptology.

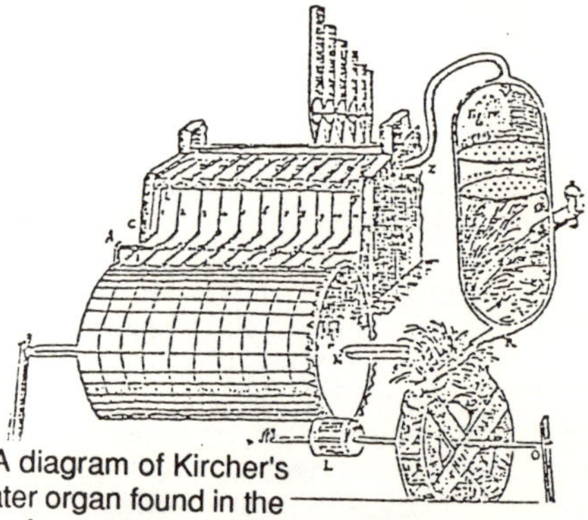

9 A diagram of Kircher's water organ found in the *Ars et Métiers* museum in Paris.

> It is therefore Kircher's incontestable merit that he was the first to have discovered the phonetic value of an Egyptian hieroglyph. From a humanistic as well as an intellectual point of view Egyptology may very well be proud of having Kircher as its founder.[20]

Since he was present at the violent eruption of Mount Etna in 1630, he had himself lowered into the cone for closer observation. It was good preparation for his two volume work, *Mundus subterraneus* (Amsterdam, 1665), probably the first printed work on geophysics and vulcanology. In it he held that much of the phenomena on earth including the formation of minerals was due to the fact that there was fire under the terra firma, an unusual teaching for those days. Some of his works were really encyclopedic in their scope. One such is *Phonurgia nova* (Kempten, 1673) which contains all the then-known mathematics and physics concerning sound and includes his invention of the megaphone. Another is the popular *Musurgia universalis* (Rome, 1646), one of his longest works, which marks a crucial juncture in the development of music.[21] He had the good sense to distribute 300 copies to the Jesuit delegates from around the world who happened to be in Rome for the Eighth General Congregation of the Jesuit Society (1645-1646) which coincided with the publication of his book.

Although he adhered to Aristotelian physics, **Kircher** had no tolerance for alchemy, which, by the way, was taken seriously by Newton and Boyle. Newton's calculus and Boyle's law were apparently enough to extricate these latter two gentlemen from the later ridicule heaped on their contemporaries who were engaged in the Hermetic arts.

Kircher's treatise on light, *Ars magna lucis et umbrae* (Rome, 1646), treats also of the planetary system. In it he shows no inclination to follow the heliocentric system, but he does favor Tycho Brahe's model in which the planets circle the sun. Some other inventions are found in this book, such as the magic lantern, the predecessor to the movies. For three centuries a science museum founded by **Kircher**, (perhaps one of the first of its kind in the world) has survived in Rome. Recently the scientific items of this museum have been divided up and spread throughout three Roman museums. So broad (and so well-known) were his interests that he was the recipient of many scientific curiosities.

One such curiosity is occasionally on display at the Yale Beinecke Rare Book Library. It is the Voynich "cipher" manuscript, probably about five hundred years old, a scientific text in an unidentified language called "the most mysterious manuscript in the world." Written by hand in an unknown alphabet on vellum it has 102 leaves including 8 folding leaves with about 400 botanical and 33 astrological subjects in five colors. Some of the plants have been identified as peculiar to America, so the earliest date would be the time of Columbus. To this day no one has been able to decipher it. One of **Kircher's** former students, John Marcus Marci, found it and brought it to Kircher because of his work on universal languages saying, ". . . for such Sphinxes as these obey no one but their master, **Kircher**." The present name of the manuscript " Voynich" is the name of the donor who was willing to pay $160,000 "for a book no one could read." It once belonged to **Athanasius Kircher** and had been on display in his museum.

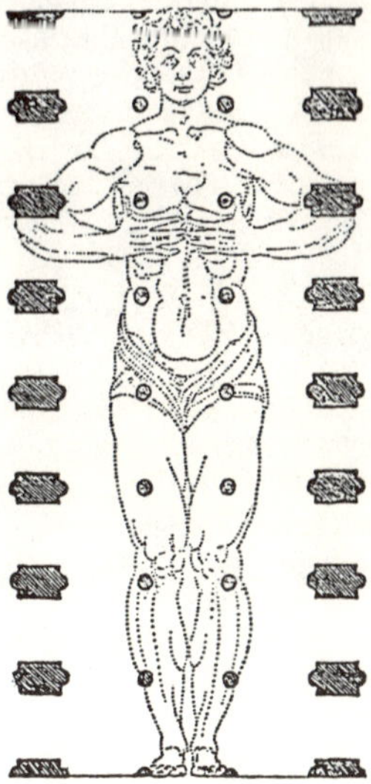

10 Kircher's anthropomorphic proportions for Noah's Arc.

As a youngster **Kircher** had three near-death experiences. While swimming in a forbidden pond he was swept under a mill wheel; later inadvertently he was pushed from an onlooking crowd into the path of race horses; and finally he suffered a gangrenous leg from a skating accident. The last cured suddenly after he prayed to the Blessed Virgin and it occurred to young **Athanasius** that he was receiving a great deal of divine protection and he did not forget these signs. In 1661 he found the remains of an ancient Marian church built by Constantine on the spot of St. Eustace's vision. He restored the place as a shrine and visited it often. Then when he died his heart was taken and buried there according to his last request.[22] It is rather remarkable that this brilliant geometer and encyclopedist, called the father of geology and of Egyptology, founder of the first public museum and skilled in so many other branches of knowledge should reveal such simple piety. **Athanasius Kircher** deserves the title given him: "Master of a Hundred Arts".

Chapter 1 Footnotes

1. Vol. X - Col. 823-831. Besides these 631 authors, many other Jesuit geometers are listed in eight other columns under different headings of "applied geometry". A more recent addition to the 44 books on the calendar and valuable source of information for this work is the book by G. Coyne,S.J., M. Hoskin and O. Pedersen: *Gregorian reform of the calendar.* Specola Vaticana, 1983.
2. J. M. Child: *The Early Mathematical Manuscripts of Leibniz.* Chicago: Open Court, 1920, p. 11-14. This letter is quoted in chapter 4.
3. Moritz Cantor:*Vorlesungen ueber Geschichte der Mathematik.* Leipsig: 1900-1908, Vol. 2, p. 512.
4. See chapter 3, concerning "Analytic geometry", for a fuller explanation.
5. Etienne Montucla: *Histoire des mathematiques.* Paris: vol 2, 1798-1799, p. 79.
6. The source of my translation is: "Lettre inédite de Christophe Grienberger sur Grégoire de Saint-Vincent" found in *Annales de la Societe d'Emulation* . vol. I, 1913, p. 50. "Dicam hic demum quod sentio: Patrem Gregorium non solum non esse dimittendum, sed potius in compedes conjiciendum, donec saltem quadraturam eo loco relinquat, quo perire amplius non possit. Ita sentio."
7. TRS, vol.3, p. 869-876.
8. TRS, vol.3, p. 874.
9. DSB, vol.1, p. 81. J. E. Morere gives a brief description of d'Aquilon's book as well as several references to histories of perspective geometry and photometry.
10. DSB vol.1 p. 81.
11. Henri Bosmans: "Le Mathématicien Anversois Jean-Charles della Faille" in *Mathesis.* vol 41, 1927, p. 5-11. Bosmans relates the life of de la Faille and describes his contributions to geometry including a reproduction of de la Faille's portrait painted by Anthony Van Dyke, now found in the Plantin Museum in Brussels. Also, ibid. p. 7n "Magnifique marque d'imprimeur de Meursius, dessinée par P. P. Rubens."
12. Lancelot White: *Roger Joseph Boscovich.* New York: Fordham, 1961, p. 14.
13. Ibid., p. 31.
14. Ibid., p. 138.
15. Ibid., p. 224.
16. Ibid., p. 183.
17. Ibid., p. 41.
18. Morris Kline: *Mathematical thought from ancient to modern times.* New York: Oxford, 1972. p. 395.
19. James Newman: *The World of Mathematics.* New York: 1956, vol.2 p. 1020n.
20. Erik Iverson: *The Myth of Egypt and its Hieroglyphs* : Copenhagen: 1961, p. 97-98.
21. Joscelyn Godwin: *Athenasius Kircher.* London: Thames and Hudson, 1979, p. 66-67.
22. Ludwig Koch ed.: *Jesuiten-Lexikon.* Waversebaan: Lowen-Heverlee, 1962, vol 2 p. 983.

Chapter 2 Inventions in Practical Geometry

The geometrical apparatus recognized by Euclid was simple: a straight edge and a compass. To apply geometry, however, to gnonomics, hydrology, perspectives, architecture, astronomy and other fields dependent on geometry, more intricate apparatus had to be invented. Some of the Jesuit geometers were quite good at this, and a few like **Francesco Lana-Terzi** and **Athanasius Kircher** were listed as inventors even though credit for their inventions was not always attributed to them. The inventions may be grouped roughly according to pure geometry, and geometry applied to other fields such as dyalling/gnomonics, astronomy, physics.

a. Inventions to simplify geometry
b. Inventions in horology/gnomonics
c. Inventions in geometrical optics
d. Inventions in physics

a. Geometry

In his *Modern Geometry*, Howard Eves[1] describes the pantograph invented by **Christopher Scheiner** used for homothetic transformations for enlarging curves. This instrument consists of parallel and intersecting rods hinged at appropriate ratio points and is found in one of the Rubens paintings in a book by Erindo Rametta.[2] It is still available in art stores today. **Thomas Ceva** invented an apparatus to divide an angle into n equal parts. This was later claimed by Guillaume l'Hospital (d 1704), who also claimed authorship of what is now known as "l'Hospital's rule" which had been discovered by his teacher John Bernoulli.

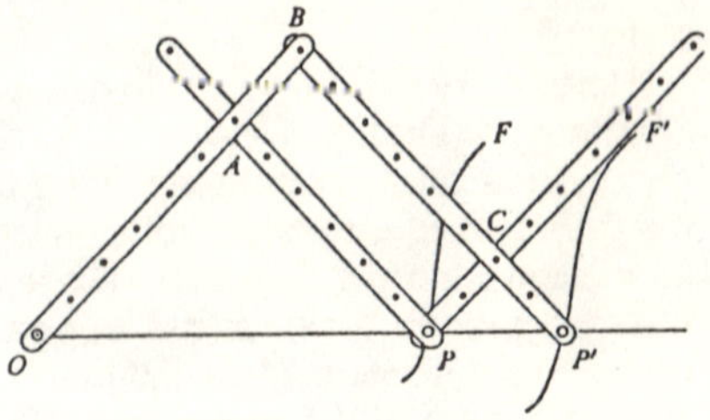

1 Scheiner's pantograph still available today in art stores.
OA = AP and PC = P'C = AB
So OP'/OP = OB/OA = k

Kircher invented what he called the *Pantometrium* for solving problems of practical geometry. He also invented the first counting machine. Both are described in *Pantometrium Kirchereanum* (Wurzburg 1669). He constructed a machine for teaching mathematical methods which could be reduced to algorithms. **Kircher**, by the way, was first to discover and report on sea phosphoresence.[3]

One of the most widely used devices found in so many instruments was invented by **Clavius.** It is called the *Vernier* scale. Some historians of science wished to change the name so it would properly be called the **Clavius** scale because it was his invention. This is related in the DSB: it started with an idea **Clavius** received from his teacher Nunez.

> Nunez's method . . .was extremely difficult to engrave with precision using a different scale on each concentric circle. Brahe remarked that in practice Nunez's method failed to live up to its promise. . . . About fifty years later **Clavius,** who had studied under Nunez, found a way to facilitate the engraving of the various scales on the concentric circular segments. . . . It thus became possible to read off degrees and minutes directly if the outer scale were divided into degrees and if there were sixty concentric circular segments. These methods were described by **Clavius** in his *Geometria practica* (Rome, 1604), which Vernier surely read and meditated on.[3]

It is well-known that Pascal constructed a calculator in 1641 made of small gears. A model of it of recent vintage is on display in the *Ars et Métiers* Museum in Paris (near a display of **Kircher's** water organ). But it is not well known that **Jean Ciermans** in his book *Repetitio Menstrua* (Louvain, 1639) described a similar calculating instrument two years earlier, which he constructed of small gears "incapable of erring."[4] **Cierman's** ideas ran a little ahead of technology, and he was not satisfied with the construction of the apparatus which he designed.[5] Later another Jesuit, Joseph Liesganig, invented a device to read tangents instead of angles and found a way to fit clocks with a micrometer screw for more accurate reading.

b. <u>Horology</u>

Horology or gnomonics, sometimes called Dyalling (Dialling), was a practical geometrical study originating in the time of the Chaldeans. It consisted of creating rules for making sundials. One such device, called the "capuchin," since its appearance resembles a cowl, is attributed to the Jesuit François de Saint Rigaud,S.J. **Gaspar Schott** wrote about these devices as did **Kircher** in his *Ars magna lucis* (Amsterdam, 1671). An 800 page work of **Clavius**, *Gnomonices* (Rome,1612), contained all that was known about gnomonics and horology at the time of publication.

In the Florence cathedral of Santa Maria is found a plaque commemorating the work of **Leonard Ximenes**, a Jesuit geometer and highway engineer (after whom is named the main road to Pistoia), for his work on the largest gnomon in the known world, which had been constructed in the 5th century.[6] **Ignace Pardies** was another geometer known for his dial designs, and the TRS thought it worth mentioning, in a review of his book, *Eléments de géométrie:*

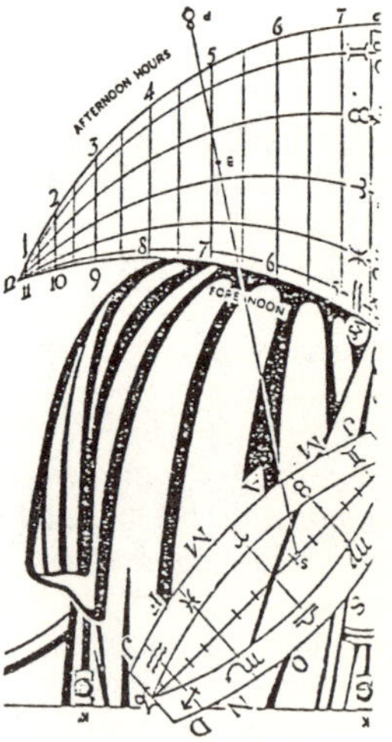

2 "Capuchin" dial designed by François de St Rigaud, S.J. -- so named because of the cowl appearance.

The Learned Author, Professor of the Mathematiques in the Parisian College of Clermont, has found the difficulty met within the Practick of Dyalling.[7]

A rather celebrated case of "dyalling" is the water clock of **Francis Line** whose construction consisted of a glass sphere floating freely inside a larger glass sphere which was filled with fluid, making one complete revolution every 24 hours. The inner sphere rotated at a regular rate throughout the day in such a way that a little fish, also floating in the fluid, pointed towards the hours of the day which were marked on a scale on the outer surface of the floating globe.[8] After constructing one at Liege and keeping its workings secret, he was asked by Nicholas Peiresc, a friend of Galileo, if he would bring it to Rome to help Galileo defend the heliocentric theory, because the unusual design was fascinating and had interesting demonstration possibilities, even for inquisitors. Although **Line** was willing, Galileo was not. Later, Hooke figured out how the mechanism worked and published it in the TRS.[9]

Line was referred to in the TRS as "**Francis Line** (alias Thomas Hall)" as if it were all one name. It was common for exiled English Jesuits to use aliases to protect their families and also help them move in and out of England with greater ease. It was, after all, a time when those who harbored Jesuits in Merry England were pressed to death while the Jesuits themselves were hanged, drawn and quartered. In spite of all this, Jesuits desired to return on any pretext and sometimes their presence was even needed by the Loyalists. In 1669 King Charles II felt he needed a sundial for his garden in Whitehall: it had to be the best dial possible, so **Francis Line** was chosen for the job. Some sort of gentleman's truce was arranged. **Line** built the dial himself, modeling it after the sundial he had built at Liege, and it was an immense success. Then he described it in Protestant England's very own periodical, the Philosophical Transactions of the Royal Society.[10] Later he published an illustrated book with the elaborate title: *An Explication of the Diall sett up in the King's Garden at London, an. 1669, by which besides the hours of all kinds diversely expressed, many things also belonging to Geography, Astrology and Astronomy are by the Sunne's shadow made known to the eye* (Liege, 1673).

The reform of the calendar was perhaps the best known Jesuit influence on time measurement. Were it not for **Christopher Clavius** we would be celebrating Christmas on 12 December solar time. In 1582, the Julian calendar ended on a Thursday, 4 October, with the promulgation of the papal bull *Inter gravissimas* (published 24 February 1582), stating that "ten days be taken away, from the third nones to the ides of October." The next day, the Gregorian calendar began on a day named Friday, 15 October (after the arbitrary fashion in which mathematicians define objects and use axioms).

3 Scheiner's apparatus for tracing sun spots. In his controversy with Galileo concerning sunspots he borrowed from Greek mythology the name *Apelles* who split the line drawn by Protogenes with a finer line. Scheiner thought the sun spots were planets.

October was chosen by **Clavius** for the conversion because it was the month with the fewest number of feast days and also seemed to promise the least interference with commerce.

The calendar change was the result of the work of a commission appointed by Pope Gregory XIII and led by **Clavius** to correct the Julian calendar. For centuries, it was known that Easter was being celebrated on the wrong day, and sometimes with an error of twenty-eight days. For about 800 years many scholars, such as Roger Bacon (and in a later century Carl F Gauss), had failed to find a formula which would identify the correct date for Easter, and also correct the Julian calendar for the future.

4 Johann Schall von Bell (1591-1666). One of three giants of the China mission.

The problem with the Julian calendar was partly astronomical and partly arithmetic. A year (the time for a complete transit of the earth around the sun) is shorter now than it was in 45 B.C., when the Julian calendar was adopted. Then the transit time was 365.2422 days; now it is 365.2419 days (a day being the time required for the sun to return to a fixed meridian). Neither of these numbers is an integer, so a year does not have an integral number of days. If a year were divided up into a number of equal days, there would be no 23rd day of the year; it would be, for instance, the 23.1368th day of the year. No one wanted this, especially printers!

In the Julian calendar, a year was taken to be 365 and l/4 days so that by adding one extra day (February 29) at the end of every fourth year (the Julian calendar began on March l), the fraction would be taken care of. It was not. The solar year could not keep up with the Julian calendar since it was was 664 seconds longer than it was supposed to have been. By 1582 the vernal equinox had drifted to March 11. Easter, therefore, shifted erratically because of its complicated dependence on the vernal equinox . This had been decreed by the council of Nicaea in 325: "the first Sunday after the date of the first full moon that occurs on or after the vernal equinox." **Clavius'** task, to calculate the time of the vernal equinox and to correct the shift, was monumental considering the meager astronomical and mathematical resources available at the time. This was long before the invention of most of the mathematical tools we take for granted today. It was a time that preceded the use of a decimal point (introduced by **Clavius**) and long division was considered a college major! The accuracy of his calculations has earned **Clavius** historical fame, and it took him 800 pages in his *Novi calendarii* (Rome, 1588) to explain and justify his results.

Of the many attempts to solve the problem, some were more precise, but required a thorough knowledge of astronomy to compute a date. Kepler, defending **Clavius'** simple plan, said: "After all, Easter is a feast, not a planet!" Joseph Scaliger, author of a competing plan, took the rejection of his plan less than gracefully and referred to **Clavius** as nothing more than a "German fat-belly." Later, in a better mood, Scaliger acknowledged his esteem for Clavius saying, "A censure from Clavius is more palatable than the praise of other men."

Implementation of the plan was not an immediate and universal success. It had a fate similar to the adoption of the metric system in America today. The populace was quite upset and windows were broken in the houses of the European Jesuits who were blamed for the change. The Orthodox Church saw it as a Roman intrusion (which it was), and Protestant countries were understandably reluctant to accept any decree from the pope. England did not adopt the Gregorian calendar until 1752, while Orthodox Russia would require the Bolshevik revolution.

It is significant that **Clavius** discovered that 97 days had to be added every 400 years and that this could be easily arranged by adding a day every four years omitting the three century years not divisible by 400. The wonder is that he was able to measure the year length so accurately that he knew the number of extra days required. To this day no one knows how he did it. It is interesting to notice that he, like all the others coping with the calendar problem, assumed a geocentric system when working on the calendar, although he later taught and became a staunch supporter of the heliocentric theory. The fact that there exist 400 unique calendars is another indicator of the complications involved: 1988 will not be exactly duplicated until 2388. A cursory review of the extensive "calendar" literature over the years illustrates that correcting the calendar was not a trivial problem.

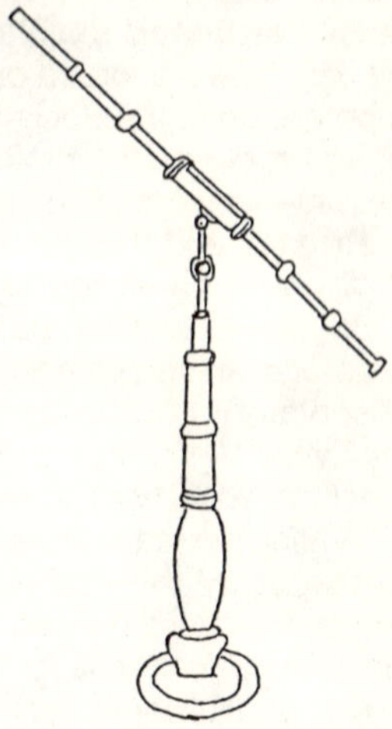

5 Schall von Bell telescope, introducing the Chinese to the refractor telescope.

c. Astronomy and Geometrical Optics

Christopher Grienberger invented the equatorial mount in which the telescope rotates about an axis which is parallel to the earth's axis.[11] It was described by **Scheiner** in his *Rosa Ursina sive Sol* (Bracciano, 1630), although he had used it as early as 1620. In 1613 **Scheiner** in turn contributed to the invention of the refracting telescope with which we are familiar today. He constructed a number of different kinds of telescopes, and in particular (perhaps at the suggestion of Kepler) he made one with two convex lenses instead of Galileo's scheme which included one concave and the other convex. This improved sightings greatly. **Scheiner** gave one of his telescopes to the archduke of Tyrol who was more interested in the scenery from his Innsbruck castle than he was in the stars. When he complained that the image was upside down, **Scheiner** inserted another lens to invert the image and so created one of the first terrestrial telescopes.[12]

Scheiner's pupil, another Jesuit geometer and astronomer, Johann Cysatus was the first to make a telescopic study of a comet in 1618 and gave the first description of the nucleus and coma of a comet. At the entrance to the moon exhibit at the

Smithsonian in Washington, D.C. is the first selenogragh of the moon with craters and mountains identified by persons' names. It was meticulously drawn by another Jesuit, **Francesco Maria Grimaldi** and was published in the *Almagestum Novum* (Bologna, 1651) of **John Baptist Riccioli**.

The Jesuit geometers and astronomers in Rome were able to gather information from their former pupils in China and India on lunar and solar eclipses and transits of Venus. The information that was gathered enabled **Riccioli** to compose a table of 2,700 selenographical objects, incomparably more accurate than anything previously known.

A recent article in New Scientist[13] concerns an astronomical observatory whose director was the Flemish Jesuit **Ferdinand Verbiest.** When the Jesuits were forced out, after the suppression of the Society, it fell into disrepair; during the Boxer Rebellion instruments were stolen and brought to Prussia and the Jesuit scientific library was given to the Czar. In 1981, however, China and Belgium negotiated an agreement to restore the observatory (the assumption being that since **Verbiest** was Flemish the Belgians would want to contribute).

6 Sketch of a European ship from Verbiest's 1672 work *Khun yu thu shuo* concerning world maps.

Among the many tasks entrusted to **Verbiest** by the Emperor was the improvement of the defense weapons. He cast 132 cannons for the imperial army, instruments far superior to any previous Chinese weapons. He also invented a more efficient type of gun carriage. When the guns were finished **Verbiest** determined to consecrate them in a public ceremony and so on each gun he engraved the name of a Christian saint. Clothed in surplice and stole, he sprinkled the cannon with holy water and offered prayers for the proper deployment of the guns, while imperial dignitaries looked on. The tests of the cannon were successful and the grateful Emperor took off his own robe and gave it to **Verbiest** in an unusual mark of imperial favor. The role of the Jesuits as cannon makers again brought down upon the Jesuit order bitter criticism from its enemies in Europe, but Pope Innocent XI sent **Verbiest** a brief (12/3/1681) praising him "for using the profane sciences for the safety of the people and for the spread of the faith." It is unlikely that such a brief would have been sent today.

The reflecting telescope was invented by **Nicolas Zucchi** in 1606, who brought one to Kepler as a gift from the Society of Jesus at the urging of another Jesuit, **Paul Guldin.** Kepler was so thrilled with it that he dedicated his last book to **Paul Guldin**.

The achromatic telescope was invented by **Boscovich**, as was the ring micrometer (although credit is sometimes given to Huygens).[14] He proposed an original theory of the double refraction occurring in Iceland Spar.[15] He did not take undue pride in his inventions but stated that he published his inventions in order to stimulate someone else to invent something better.[16]

d. Physics

Francesco Grimaldi discovered the diffraction of light and gave it the name *diffraction*, which means "breaking up." He laid the groundwork for the later invention of the diffraction grating. **Louis Castel** invented an ocular harpsichord which makes colors and musical tones correspond. Capillary dispersion was discovered by **Honoré Fabri** who also gave the first reasonable explanation of why the sky is blue.

Francesco Lana-Terzi is found at the head of literature on Aviation because of the treatise in his book *Prodromo alla Arte Maestra* (1670) on aerostatics.[17] His work was translated by Robert Hooke and presented to the Royal Society of London by Robert Boyle. Later it was discussed by physicists for over a century before the first successful aerostatics flight by the Montgolfier brothers in 1783. His work fascinated scientists because it was the first time anyone worked out the geometry and physics for such a device. Instead of putting something *into* a balloon as we do today he would take the air *out.* **Lana-Terzi's** treatise had five principles.

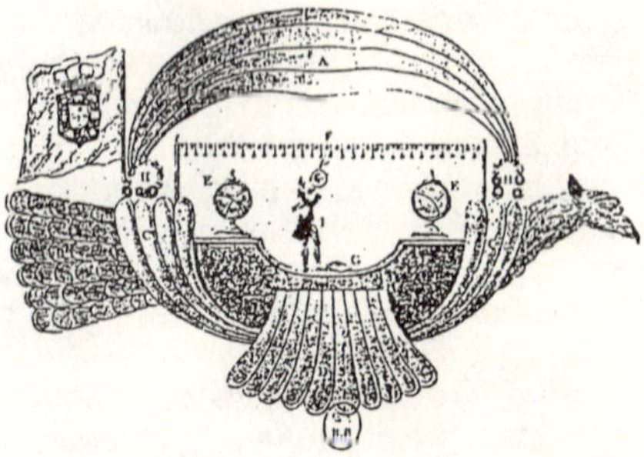

7 Unsuccessful hot air balloon of Lourenço de Gusmâo, S.J.which set fire to the kings palace, "who fortunately did not take it ill".

1. Air has weight as Boyle's pump proves.
2. This weight can be calculated.
3. Nearly all air can be exhausted from any vessel, as in animal respiration.
4. From Euclid we know that while the area of a sphere depends on the square of the diameter, the volume depends on its cube, so that if a sphere has a large enough area it can hold a predetermined mass of air inside.
5. Finally, from Archimedes we know that lighter bodies float in denser fluids.

From the latter **Lana-Terzi** concludes that one could construct a vessel which would weigh less than the air within and so when the air had been pumped out the whole would float in the atmosphere. In fact if the vessel were made large enough it could support the weight of a ship with passengers. After he had calculated the weights and volumes involved, the vessel he proposed consisted of four large twenty five foot spheres made of thin sheet copper bound together and supporting a basket for the riders, with a sail and rudder for steering.

After a long discussion of these principles **Lana-Terzi** answers the objections to his proposal. First, the problem of evacuating the air could be accomplished by Boyle's pump. A second objection was that the airship was liable to float off into outer space so that the riders would not be able to breathe. **Lana-Terzi** shows unusual grasp of aerostatics for that time by replying that the ship would stop rising as soon as the density of the atmosphere counterbalanced the weight of the ship.

Landing the craft once it is airborne is guaranteed by installing a valve to let air into the four spheres as ballast which would bring the ship back down to earth. The sail and a large rudder would take care of steering the ship so that it would not be blown away. Later experiments proved that a sail would not be an effective steering device. The most serious problem **Lana-Terzi** addresses and the one most scientists noticed was the fact that the spheres would be crushed by the atmosphere when the air was pumped out. **Lana-Terzi's** answer was clever but inadequate. He thought that the spherical shape would prevent it from being crushed because of the perfect uniformity of a sphere, somewhat as an eggshell is not easily broken when surrounded by uniform pressure when held properly in the palm of one's hand. He happened to be wrong in solving this last problem, and so his proposed ship never did succeed. His expectation of landing ease was too optimistic also: "There is no need for ports since the balloon could land anywhere." **Lana-Terzi's** treatment was remarkably thorough for an era when experimental data was quite scarce. Berbardo Zamaga was inspired to write a poem concerning **Lana-Terzi's** *"Navis Aeria".* Some 39 years later another Jesuit Bartholomeu Lourenço de Gusmâo, S.J. from Brazil attempted to use hot air under a kind of umbrella, supporting a basket for riders, in the presence of the king of Portugal (who paid for the experiment). He momentarily got off the ground but in doing so set fire to a part of the king's house. "Fortunately the king did not take it ill," an onlooker later wrote.

Lana-Terzi's influence on speculation for flight was of long duration. For a century it was studied and discussed by scientists such as Sturm, who had great praise for the plan, and by Leibniz who verified **Lana-Terzi's** calculations. **Lana-Terzi** answered the many objections but failed to recognize the crushing force of the atmosphere on the supporting balloons, in fact, in his time no one else did either. Lana never built the machine for two reasons: one was that, because of his vow of poverty, he did not have the 2,000 ducats necessary, and secondly, he felt that God would never allow the machine to succeed, because it would lead to aerial bombardment. At least in the latter he was right. It only took l0 years after the Montgolfier brothers flight for the French Navy to adopt balloons as warships.

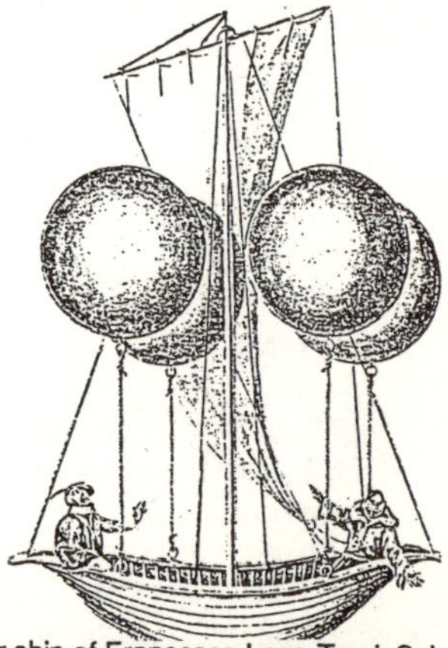

8 Air ship of Francesco Lana-Terzi, S.J. A model was constructed by the Royal Society of London, and Lana's theory was discussed by physicists for a century before the first successful balloon flight.

The sentiment of the time was enthusiasm for flying, be it for pleasure, for honor or "for profit and the benefit of mankind." **Lana-Terzi** alone, so much a scientist and a man of his own century saw the possible destruction of mankind. It is ironic then that he is called *"the father of Aviation."*

Lana-Terzi also discovered a way to grow seedless fruit, and in his book *Prodromo* is found a large collection of inventions. For these reasons, he is listed by Stern as an inventor along with Torricelli and Huygens. Also, it would explain why the Royal Society adopted him as a regular contributor along with Newton and Boyle.

A book company's advertisement concerning a recent reprint of **Lana-Terzi**'s *Prodromo* describes this remarkable book reprinted over and over for more than three centuries. "The original work was found among some very rare volumes . . . a comprehensive work of inventions by Father Lana of Brescia. . .which was reprinted separately in view of the valuable and interesting nature of the subject matter. . . for the erudite reader."

In *Ars magnesia* **Kircher** described a device for measuring magnetic power by means of a balance. Later, he carefully compiled measurements of magnetic declination from several places around the world, as reported by Jesuit scholars, and particularly by his disciple Martin Martini (d 1638), who in a letter suggested the possibility of determining longitudes by the declination of a magnetic needle.[18]

Chapter 2 Footnotes

1. Howard Eves: *Modern Geometry.* Boston: 1972, p. 107.
2. Conor Reilly: *Studia Kircheriana.* Wiesbaden-Rom: Edizioni del Mondo, 1974, p. 78.
3. DSB vol.13, p. 622.
   Brahe's remark can be found in *Astronomiae instauratae mechanica.* Nuremberg: 1611, p. 2.
4. Joseph E. Hofmann: *History of mathematics.* Translated from the German by Frank Gaynor & Henrietta Midonick. New York: Philosophical Library, 1957, p. 114.
5. D.E. Smith: *History of Mathematics.* New York: Dover, p. 203.
6. Rufus Suter. "Leonard Ximenes and the Gnomon" in *ISIS* vol 55, p. 79
7. TRS vol 7, p. 5150.
8. Conor Reilly: *Francis Line, S.J. An Exiled English Scientist.* Rome: Institutum Historicum, 1969, p 27.
9. Ibid., p.33.
10. TRS vol 23, p. 1416-1418.
11. A. G. Debus: *World Who's Who in Science.* Chicago: Marquis, 1968.
    Also see: Sherwood Taylor, *A short history of science and scientific thought.* New York: Norton, 1949, p. 97.
12. Daniel O'Connell: "Jesuit Men of Science" in *Studies in Irish Literature and Science* vol 44, 1955, p. 313.
13. G. E. Beekeman: "New glory for the ancient Beijing observatory" in *New Scientist.* 20 Sept. 1984, p. 54.
14. Lancelot White: *Roger Joseph Boscovich.* New York: Fordham, 1961 p. 195n.
15. Ibid., p. 194, 195.
16. Ibid., p. 196.
17. M. Zanfredini: "Un gesuita scienziato del 600:" in *La Civiltà Cattolica* 18 luglio 1987, p. 115-128.
18. DSB vol.7, p. 375.

Chapter 3 Innovations in Geometry

A late 16th-century geometer would notice the maturing of Euclidean geometry, then some applications to trigonometry as well as to gnomonics and steriometry. The 17th-century geometers witnessed the unfolding of analytic geometry as well as the infinitesimal geometry which preceded the calculus. Finally the early 18th century would see the use of geometry, as the calculus evolved. At this time, too, the seeds were sown for future projective and non-Euclidean geometries. Jesuits were involved in all these developments. Here 9 topics are considered:

a. Euclidean geometry
b. Geometry applied to gnomonics, mapmaking, military art, architecture
c. Trigonometry
d. Analytic geometry
e. Geometry, predecessor to calculus
 1. Infinitesimals/infinite series
 2. Area under a hyperbola
 3. Center of gravity
 4. Guldin's rule
 5. Other quadratures
f. Geometry as Calculus Evolved
g. Non -Euclidean geometry
h. Projective geometry
i. Geometry applied to physics

a. <u>Euclidean geometry</u>

Clavius's *Euclidis elementorum libri XV* (Rome, 1574) contains the books of Euclid and a vast collection of comments and elucidations. Later editions of this work became the standard text for many schools of the time. **Clavius'** emphasis was not merely a spatial exercise; instead, this book on Euclidean geometry was an important step in bringing rigor to geometry. The fact that today Euclidean geometry is the most rigorous course in school mathematics is due in part to this effort of **Clavius**, who emphasized rigor in his geometry texts.

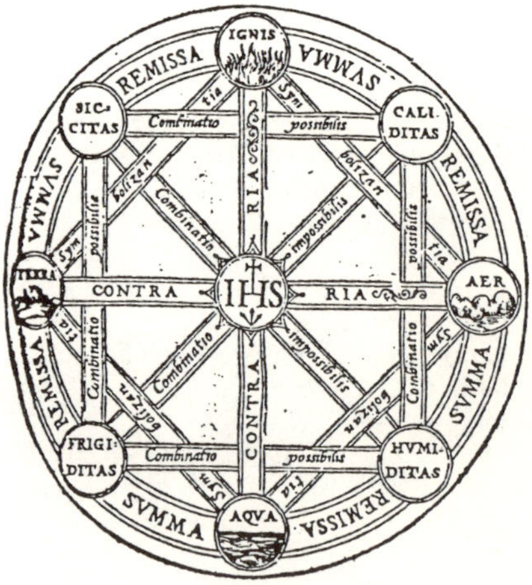

1 A page of Clavius' *Sacrobosco* showing the Jesuit Society's monogram IHS as well as the interrelations among the four phlogiston elements, earth, air, fire and water.

Clavius' treatment of synthetic geometry was not just a translation of Euclid, but a critical evaluation of Euclid's axioms[1] and included some necessary axioms that Euclid had missed. **Clavius** used a first-century method of proof which derives a proposition by assuming the contrary of the proposition to be proven. This method applied to a proposition P consists of using the fact that{[*not P implies P*]*implies P*} and is equivalent to using {[*P or P*] *implies P* }. This process for example would be used to prove that there are an infinite number of prime numbers. He also showed his appreciation for Euclid's insight that the fifth postulate was necessary, which was not a very popular opinion among l6th- and17th-century geometers. Many thought that it was either an unnecessary postulate or a very involuted theorem.

Clavius' innovations were also seen in the symbols attributed to him by Florian Cajori[2] and others, such as the radical sign, plus and minus signs, parentheses and decimal point. He proposed a proof that there can be no more than three dimensions in geometry: it was based on the fact that only three concurrent lines can be drawn from a point so that they are mutually perpendicular.[3]

Clavius' commentary on Euclid became the standard textbook for the 17th century and his books on arithmetic, geometry, algebra, harmonics and astronomy were used in all the European Jesuit schools, making him the mathematics instructor of Catholic Europe as well as much of Protestant Europe. Some of **Clavius'** students spread this new emphasis, - men such as **Matteo Ricci** who translated **Clavius'** work into Chinese, giving China its first opportunity to enjoy Euclid.

2 Matteo Ricci, S.J. (1552-1610) who translated Clavius' *Euclid* into Chinese. He was the subject of the best seller *The Memory Palace of Matteo Ricci* by Jonathan Spence.

Clavius discovered and proved a theorem for a regular polygon which has an odd (**2n+1**) number of sides. In the isosceles triangle formed by a vertex and its opposite side the base angle is **n** times the summit angle. He proved it by inscribing the polygon inside a circle. So for a pentagon (n = 2) it would be twice the summit angle, while in a 17-sided regular polygon (n = 8) the base angle of such a triangle would be 8 times the summit angle. Two centuries later Carl Friedrich Gauss would use this to construct a 17-sided regular polygon by ruler and compass and thus solve the binomial equation $\mathbf{x^{17}-1 = 0}$[4]. This was his first important mathematical discovery to be followed by an incredible number of discoveries later on.

Many other Jesuit geometers contributed to the modernization of Euclidean geometry. There are examples such as **François d'Aguilon** who proposed his own synthesis of Euclid, **Jean Villalpando** of Spain who applied the emphasis on proportions to harmonics, and **Gregory St. Vincent** who is partly responsible for the use of the equal sign as well as the practice of lettering the vertices of a polygon.

b. <u>Geometry applied to gnomonics, map-making, military art, architecture</u>

A geometer who wrote for structural and hydraulic engineers was the German Jesuit, **Johann Helfenzrieder.** He authored very accurate almanacs and then later published dissertations on the use of telescopes in astronomy and the construction of surveying apparatus. His later works include practical mechanics for structural engineers and also the study of hydraulics.

John B Riccioli went beyond the preliminary work of Galileo and succeeded in perfecting the pendulum as an instrument to measure time, thereby laying the groundwork for a number of important later applications. He also made many significant astronomical measurements in an effort to expand and refine existing data. He made measurements, for example, to determine the radius of the earth and to establish the ratio of water to land on its surface. His recourse to a geometrical treatment of these problems is noteworthy.

In 1651 one of the earliest lunar maps was published by **Riccioli** in his large work *Almagestum Novum* (Bologna, 1651), mentioned earlier. His chapter concerning the moon contains two large maps (28 cm in diameter), one of which shows for the first time the effects of librations and introduces new lunar nomenclature. He started the practice of naming lunar objects after well-known personalities (not all scientists) and almost all of these are still in use today.[5]

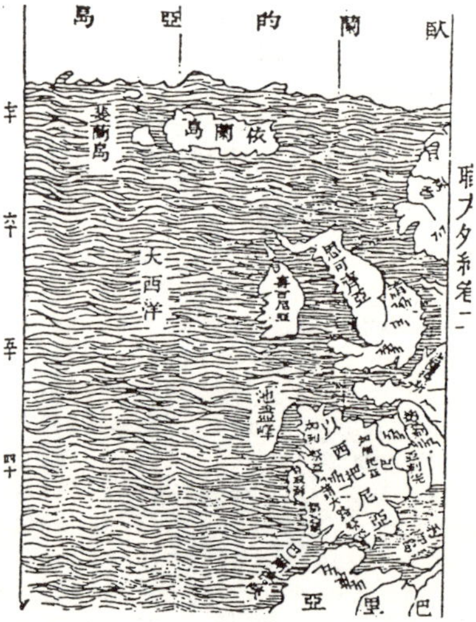

3 A map of Europe made by Jesuits for the Chinese showing parts of western Europe and giving the Chinese their first glimpse of the 'other world'.

4 Grimaldi's selenograph published by Riccioli and found at the Smithsonian entrance to the moon exhibit. Inscribed on it are the words "man does not inhabit the moon and souls do not go there."

Matteo Ricci's contributions to geography were his calculation of the breadth of China, which was three-quarters of the breadth assumed by Western geographers. Also he identified China and Peking with the Cathay and Cambaluc of Marco Polo.[6] At the time **Ricci's** maps of China were considered more accurate even than the contemporary maps of Europe. He shares the latter recognition with another Jesuit Coadjutor Brother, Benedetto de Goes, S.J., who made a journey from India to China during the years 1602-1605, in order to verify that China and Cathay were the same.[7]

The Jesuits long had an interest to find an overland route from Europe through

Christian Russia. The Tsar's ambassador to China at the time, named Spathary, was able to speak Latin and so could converse with the Jesuits. This involved **Ferdinand Verbiest** in negotiations over the border between the two countries; later it was partly under his direction that the Russo-Chinese borders were determined, and it was his surveyors who were sent out to mark them. It did not, however, put an end to border disputes, and for the past three centuries these borders continue to be contested.

Besides his numerous maps of China as well as the then-known world, **Verbiest** wrote no less than 30 books. Among these may be found a 32-volume handbook on astronomy, a Manchurian grammar, a Chinese liturgical manual and a work entitled *Kiao-li-siang-kiai,* which is a statement of the fundamental teachings of Christianity and which became the basis for later Chinese Christian literature.

It may have been noticed in Chapter 1 that a disproportionate number of books (74) concern military fortifications. The French Jesuit **Claude F M de Chales** is one of the many authors. At this time siege warfare had become a precise science depending very much on geometry. Some geometers were so good at this that they could predict precisely how many days it would take to break a siege. The fortifications had triangular shapes to protect the walls and make the weapons more effective. The offense, on the other hand, would dig three rows of trenches. The first would be cut roughly parallel to the walls but outside the range of the defending weapons; here the attacking army would mass. The next two trenches would be dug at the best possible angles to avoid the weapons while getting as close as possible to the walls as soon as possible. Since wars were continuous this science received a great deal of attention.

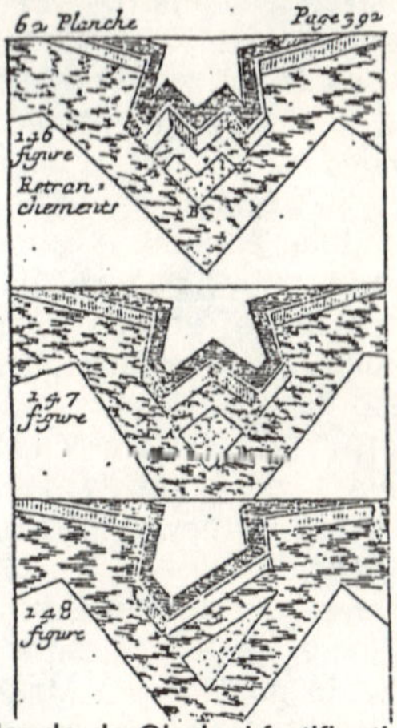

5 Claude de Chales' fortifications for defense showing abutments at various angles for greater effectiveness in neutralizing a triple tier of trenches dug by attackers.

Another Jesuit, whose contribution of geometrical designs in architecture were evident in the architectural works of Newton, was **Jean Villalpando,** who studied geometry and architecture under Juan de Herrera, the royal architect of the Spanish king Philip II. As a young man he became obsessed with the temple of Solomon and the temple described by the prophet Ezekiel. After entering the Society this interest, shared with another Jesuit, Jerome Prado, S.J., led both to collaborate in the exegesis of the prophet Ezekiel. Because of this **Villalpando** is remembered in Sommervogel for his exegetical work instead of for his contribution to the applications of geometry to architecture. That he was more than a theorist is evident from the fact that at the age of 27 while still an unordained Jesuit scholastic, he was in charge of constructing three major Jesuit buildings, one of which still stands, the church of the Jesuit college in Seville. He designed the first oval church ever built in Spain. In the history of architecture he is most renowned, however, for his famous work, the design and reconstruction of the temple of Solomon. Philip II had granted

3,000 scudi for engraving the prints. When the exegetical question arose whether Ezekiel's temple was the one Solomon built, the Jesuit General Aquaviva involved himself in the project as did Pope Sixtus V, who appointed a commission to investigate **Villalpando's** orthodoxy. The result was that Villalpando was completely cleared of misrepresenting Sacred Scripture. A study in Baroque art illustrates how **Villalpando's** *Ezechielis explicatio* (1596-1604) combines mysticism and science.[8]

Villalpando had undertaken to provide the world with the first full-scale *imago* of the Temple on the grounds that only by translating Ezechiel's vision into terms of real architecture could one fully apprehend its mystical import. The form and proportions of the Temple, which necessarily had to be perfect, since they were inspired by the Almighty Himself, provided an insight into the perfection of the City of God.

In this context it should not be forgotten how deeply the traditional concept of the Temple of Solomon as the forerunner of the celestial Jerusalem was rooted in the Jesuit Society's early history. In 1523 the founder Ignatius Loyola had undertaken the long and hazardous journey to the Holy Land, and had seen the earthly Jerusalem with his own eyes. It is recorded that, while he was there, he was seized with a burning desire to convert the Moslems. His impulse may well have stemmed from the conviction so widespread at the time that the conquest of the terrestrial Jerusalem, by either evangelization or force of arms, would be closely followed by the reign of Christ upon earth.

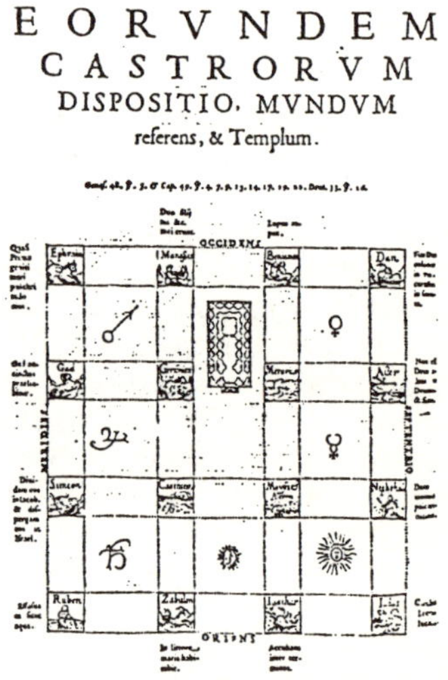

6 Villalpando's organization of Solomon's temple.

Compared to the complex task which Villalpando had been compelled to face in determining the form and dimensions of the Temple, his design was simplicity itself. According to the book of Genesis, Noah's Ark was 300 cubits long, 50 cubits wide and 30 high. Much, of course, depended on the precise value to the cubit. Origen had claimed that it was equivalent to six Roman feet, which Kircher dismissed as absurd since it would have made the Ark inordinately vast. Villalpando had maintained that it was about two and a half feet, basing his claim on the authority of Vitruvius, whereas Kircher, likewise arguing from Vitruvius, had come to the conclusion that it was one and a half feet.

The truth is that Villalpando, like his master Herrera, was one of those ambivalent figures who succeeded in having a foot in both camps. It is the same combination of the mystical and the practical that characterized men such as Copernicus, Cardanus, Tycho, Porta, John Dee, Kepler, Leibniz, and even Newton himself. So, in the Jesuit's work there seems to have been something for everyone. In 1626 Father Marin Mersenne, that inveterate enemy of everything Hermetic, drew the attention of the scholarly world to what he considered to be the innovatory nature of Villalpando's remarks on the center of gravity in his third book.

c. Trigonometry

Clavius in his three books: *Astrolabium, geometria practica,* and *Triangula sphaerica,* summarized all contemporary knowledge of plane and spherical trigonometry. Carl Boyer credits **Clavius**, "the Jesuit friend of Kepler," with the early use of the decimal point in 1593, twenty years before it became common.[9] He used it in his tables of sines. He also introduced parentheses to express aggregates. His *prosthaphaeresis* (Greek for addition and subtraction), the grandparent of logarithms, relied on the sine of the sum and differences of numbers.[10] In this way he was able to substitute addition and subtraction for multiplication, by solving the identity which we are familiar with today:

7 Villalpando's version of the sanctuary of Solomon's temple which invited an investigation by the Inquisition.

$$2 \sin x \sin y = \cos(x-y)-\cos(x+y).$$

> All computational problems involving sines, tangents and secants can be solved merely by prosthaphaeresis, that is addition and subtraction, without the laborious multiplication and division of numbers.[11]

Clavius in his *Astrolabium* credits Raymarus Ursus with the discovery of the theorem but perhaps he was being unnecessarily generous. It was **Clavius** who proved the theorem in all three forms and it was he who published it in its complete form. D. E. Smith gives the details of the proof as well as this history of its development. He emphasizes the impact **Clavius'** work had on the discovery of logarithms.

> Christopher Clavius extended the method to the cases of secants and tangents; in fact he showed how to find the product of any two numbers by this method, . . . Both fragments are from his Astrolabium (Rome 1593), Book I, lemma 53 . . . The bearing of the subject upon the theory, if not the invention, of logarithms is apparent.[12]

Clavius was one of the first to use a symbol for an unknown quantity, and although, at that time, negative solutions were not considered valid, he gave a geometric proof that the equation $\mathbf{x^2 + a = bx}$ can be satisfied by two answers. The first to establish the essential equations of spherical trigonometry was another Jesuit geometer, **Roger Boscovich.**[13]

Matteo Ricci introduced trigonometry to China, and **Ricci's** successors, **Verbiest** and **Schall von Bell**, then used the geometric and trigonometric concepts to bring about a revolution in the sciences of astronomy, the design of astronomical instruments,[14] mapmaking, and the intricate art of making accurate calendars. The Chinese celestial calendar, used to predict eclipses and comets, had been used for 40 centuries and was in desperate need of revision. **Schall von Bell** wrote no less than 150 treatises in Chinese on the calendar. Besides calendars, the Jesuits were inveterate mapmakers and were continually traveling around the empire, even though travel conditions were quite primitive. The TRS recounts 52 journeys by **Ricci** and **Verbiest** alone.

d <u>Analytic geometry</u>

Greek geometers such as Apollonius used a nonorthogonal coordinate system to solve conics and the ancient geometers knew how to fix the position of a point using coordinates. But before analytic geometry could assume its present practical form, it had to await the development of algebraic symbolism. Credit for initiating modern analytic geometry is given to Descartes and Fermat, since it was not until after their impetus that we find analytic geometry in the form with which we are familiar. Descartes' contribution is found in the appendix to his famous philosophical treatise *Discours de la méthode* (1637) while Fermat's contribution is found in his letters, some of which were to Jesuit geometers.

Gottfried Leibniz credits a Jesuit geometer in the development of analytic geometry, **Gregory St. Vincent.** In his work *Opus geometricum quadraturae circuli et sectionum coni* (1647) **Gregory St. Vincent's** treatment of conics earns him the honor of being classed by Leibniz with Fermat and Descartes as one of the founders of analytic geometry.[15]

This *Opus geometricum* has four books: first, concerning circles, triangles and transformations; then geometric sums and the Zeno paradoxes with trisection of angles using infinite series; third the conic sections; and finally, his quadrature method, based on his "ductus plani in planum" method. The latter is a summation process using a method of indivisibles, in which **St. Vincent** introduces his "virtual parabolas."

The Greeks described a spiral using an angle and a radius vector, but it was **St. Vincent** and Cavalieri who simultaneously and independently introduced them as a separate coordinate system. In an article *The Origin of polar coordinates*, J. J. Coolidge refers to the priority dispute between Cavalieri and **St. Vincent** over their discovery. **St. Vincent** wrote about this new coordinate system in a letter to **Grienberger** in 1625 and published the process in 1647. On the other hand Cavalieri's publication appeared in 1635 and the corrected version in 1653.[16]

Because invention of the calculus deflected geometrical interest away from the conics, it was not until the mid-18th century that interest in them revived, and this is partly due to the influence of **Boscovich.**[17] His treatment of conics is found in the third volume of his *Elementa* where he introduced his *eccentric circle*, now called a generating circle. Another **Boscovich** contribution to analytic geometry is clarification of the concept of continuity. The earliest thorough and geometrical treatment of the subject (continuity) is found in **Boscovich's** Appendix to his *Sectionum Conicarum Elementa.*

> In a remarkable appendix, Boscovich brings out very clearly . . . the notions of positive and negative in direction; of geometrical continuity . . . of certain properties which follow from properties of the ellipse by change of sign . . . This principle, so clearly foreshadowed by Boscovich, was seized by the great geometers of the following century, Brianchon (d 1864), Ponçelet (d 1867) and Plucker (d 1868). It may be said that as a result of Boscovich's investigations, the study of the conics reached a higher level than it had ever done before.[18]

Boscovich's interests also led him to write on the ovals of Descartes, cycloids, the logistic curve, logarithms of negative numbers, limits of certainty in astronomical investigations, and inequalities in terrestrial gravitation. In a three-year expedition he surveyed the length of two degrees of the meridian between Rome and Rimini. When he wrote his report *De litteraria expeditione* (Rome, 1755) he presented a method of adjusting arc measurement. It was the first work where probability was applied to the theory of errors. He was the precursor of Pierre Laplace,[19] who acknowledged his debt to **Boscovich** for his work in statistical analysis. Euler, Simpson and Jacobi were also indebted to **Boscovich** for his pioneering work.[20]

8 A Rubens painting showing d'Aguilon's invention, predecessor to the photometer.

e. Geometry predecessor to calculus

1. Infinitesimals/infinite series

Carl Boyer has a fine treatment of the thorny problems that had to be faced before the articulation of calculus was possible: one such problem was infinity and infinitesimals.[21] The former problem has theological implications, since nervous churchmen felt it was an intrusion into God's infinity. Cantor found this out in a later century and went to the Jesuit (non-mathematician) John Cardinal Franzelin for help in selling his ideas on infinite numbers. As a result, the strange term (a compromise) "transfinite" was introduced; it satisfied the nervous churchmen as well as the anxious mathematicians. Dirk Struik speaks of a similar problem at the time of **Gregory St. Vincent** and **André Tacquet**, when the groundwork was being laid for the infinitesimal calculus. Aristotle and Aquinas held that there is no actual infinite and a continuous line cannot be made up of indivisible parts. A point could generate a line by motion but a point was not part of a line.

> . . . Georg Cantor has remarked that the transfinitum cannot be more energetically

desired and cannot be more perfectly determined and defended than was done by St Augustine . . . Such speculations had their influence on the inventors of the infinitesimal calculus in the seventeenth century and on the philosophers of the transfinite in the nineteenth; Cavalieri, Tacquet, Bolzano and Cantor knew the scholastic authors and pondered over the meaning of their ideas.[22]

9 A Rubens painting showing one of d'Aguilon's projections of the globe held by Atlas.

Kepler listed volumes whose volume formulas were unknown and Cavalieri in his *Geometria indivisibilibus* (1635) explained a process for finding many of these volumes by using indivisibles. Though easy to use and yielding correct results most of the time, Cavalieri's method lacked a mathematical foundation; but, since it worked, it remained in use for about fifty years. **Paul Guldin** criticized Cavalieri's use of indivisibles because they lacked rigor and led to fallacies. If a line has no width then the addition of any number of lines can never yield an area, just as an infinite number of planes with no thickness cannot form a solid. Furthermore if a solid is made up of an infinite number of sections with no thickness, then these elements cannot even be compared with one another. **Guldin** also was the chief critic of Kepler in his use of infinitesimals for analogous reasons: in both cases there was a lack of rigor and mathematical foundation.

Andre Tacquet was another who would not admit Cavalieri's method to be either legitimate or geometrical. A sphere was not made up of circles nor a wedge made up of triangles but rather a volume must be composed of *homogenea*, parts of like dimensions, that is, solids of small solids and areas of small areas. **Tacquet** used the method of exhaustion and pointed the way to the limit process, and his ideas later exerted an influence on Roberval and Fermat. **Tacquet** was a brilliant mathematician of international reputation as well as a fine author. His *Opera mathematica* and his two textbooks on *Geometry* and *Arithmetic* were reprinted and translated often and were used throughout Europe during the seventeenth and eighteenth centuries.

Although **Tacquet** was born a century before Newton published his calculus, he helped articulate some of the preliminary concepts necessary for Newton and Leibniz to recognize the inverse nature of the quadrature and the tangent. He described how a moving point could generate a curve and he treated area and volume in his major work *Cylindricorum et annularium* (Antwerp, 1651). This work influenced the thinking of Pascal and his contemporaries.

Gregory St. Vincent was one of the pioneers of infinitesimal analysis.[23]
In his *Opus geometricum* (1649) he proposed a new ingenious method of approaching the problem of infinitesimals and he gave his propositions a direct rigorous demonstration instead of the *reductio ad absurdum* argument used previously. **St. Vincent** added an element not previously found in geometrical

works because he connected the question with the philosophical discussions of continuum and the result of the infinite division. George Sarton refers to this obliquely, while discussing the esoteric nature of mathematics compared with other sciences; the historical treatment has to be different.[24]

St. Vincent summed infinitely thin rectangles to find a volume by a process he called "ductus plani in planum" (multiplication of a plane into a plane). It is practically the same fundamental principle as today's present method of finding a volume of a solid of integration. The cubature of a solid bounded by two plane laminas would be obtained by constructing thin rectangles perpendicular to both laminas whose sum would equal the volume. Let **OXYZ** be the volume enclosed by a conic surface with **OX** the axis and **XYZ** the base. Consider an arbitrary, variable section **xyz // XYZ** and also perpendicular to **OXZ.** Let **xx'** be the altitude of a rectangle equal in area to the section **xzy.** The volume of the figure is found by multiplying this variable **xx'**, as it moves from **O** to **X**, by the breadth of the section **OXZ** and then adding the results.[25]

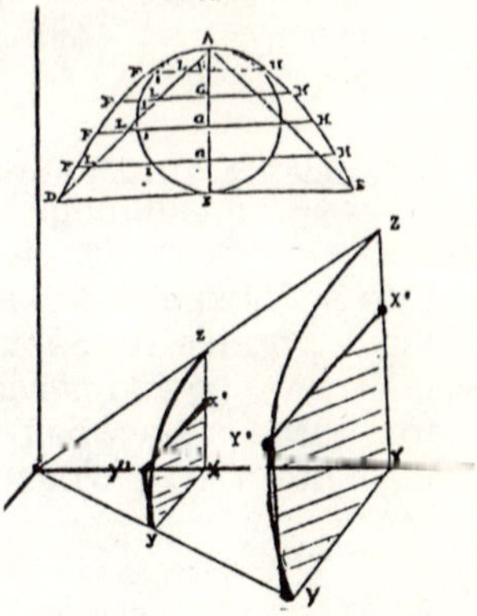

10 Gregory St.Vincent's "ductus plani in planum", a method for finding volumes before calculus was invented, which anticipated multiple integration methods used today. The cross-section xyz equals the rectangular area xx'yy'.

St. Vincent applied his process to many such solids and found the volumes. He differed from Cavalieri's method since his laminas "exhaust" the body within which they are inscribed: they have some thickness. This was a new use of this term since it literally does "exhaust" the volume instead of finding the volume to some predetermined accuracy. While **St. Vincent** was not clear how to visualize the process, he certainly was nearer to the modern view than any of his predecessors. This led him to the concept of a limit of an infinite geometrical progression which ultimately supplies the rigorous basis for the calculus. **St. Vincent** gave the first explicit statement that an infinite series can be defined by a definite magnitude which we now call its limit.

> St. Vincent was probably the first to use the word *exhaurire* in a geometrical sense. From this word arose the name "method of exhaustion" . . . he used a method of transformation of one conic to another, which contains germs of analytic geometry. St. Vincent permitted the subdivisions to continue *ad infinitum* and obtained a geometric series that was infinite. . . . He was first to apply geometric series to the "Achilles". . . moreover was first to state the exact time and place of overtaking the tortoise.[26]
>
> The terminus of a progression is the end of the series which the progression never reaches, even if continued to infinity, but to which it can approach more closely than by any given interval.[27]

St. Vincent in Book II of *Opus geometricum* applies his infinite-series process to Zeno's Achilles paradox and is perhaps the first to do so successfully. Boyer's comment on the efforts of St. Vincent and his unfortunate assumption that he had squared the circle:

> Although St. Vincent did not express himself with the rigor and clarity of the nineteenth century, his work is to be kept in mind as the first attempt explicitly to formulate in a positive sense-although still in geometrical terminology-the limit doctrine, which had been implicitly assumed by both Stevin and Valerio, as also, probably, by Archimedes in his method of exhaustion. He maintained that he had squared the circle . . . and received disdain from his contemporaries, his memory being rehabilitated by Huygens and Leibniz. On the other hand there can be no doubt that his work exerted a strong influence on many of the mathematicians of his time.[28]

2. <u>Area under a hyperbola</u>

Another breakthrough in the preparation for the calculus was due in part to **St. Vincent** and to another Jesuit, **Alphonse de Sarasa**.[29] It was discovering and proving that the area between the hyperbola and its asymptote is a logarithmic relation.[30]

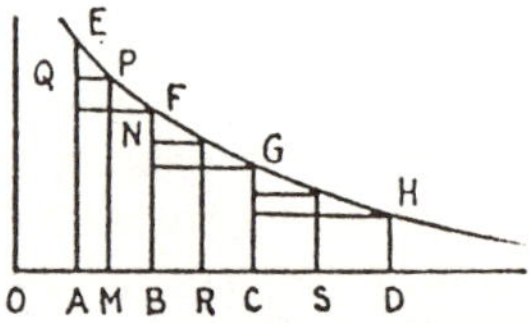

11 Discovery of Sarasa and St. Vincent: The area under a hyperbola is a logarithmic relation and is the limit of a converging series of rectangular areas.

> By inscribing and circumscribing rectangles in a geometric series in and about a hyperbola, Gregorius developed a quadrature of a segment bound by two asymptotes, a line parallel to one of them, and the portion of the curve contained between the two parallels. The relation between this procedure and logarithms was first noticed by Alfonso de Sarasa.[31]

The reasoning of **Sarasa** and **St. Vincent** focused on the fact that the area under the hyperbola from **1** to **x** plus the area from **1** to **y** equals the area from **1** to **xy.** The geometric progression $\mathbf{1/1-x = 1+x+x^2+x^3+\dots}$ where the left side is a hyperbola whose area can be determined by the method of Archimedes and the right side is the logarithmic series according to the definition of Napier's logarithm.

> . . . Just at this time a most important discovery was made concerning this case by the Jesuit Gregorius St. Vincent . . . at the end of his formidably bulky opus on geometry. . . concerning the quadrature of the circle, which so discredited his opus that those excellent discoveries at the end were almost overlooked. . . . This was the discovery that the area under the equilateral hyperbola is exactly the logarithm of Napier. Only the proof was yet missing that this was the "natural" logarithm to the base **e**.[32]

3. <u>Center of gravity</u>

Another contributor to preparations for calculus was **Charles de la Faille** who owed his fame as a scholar to his tract *Theoremata de centro gravitatis partium circuli et ellipsis* (Antwerp, 1632), in which the center of gravity of a sector of a circle is determined for the first time. His contribution is briefly described here and can be found in DSB,[33] which is the same as the essay of Henry Bosmans "Le Mathematicien Anversois."[34] His method to find the center of gravity of a circular sector anticipates a limit process. He shows that if B is sufficiently small the length $\mathbf{R\ A^2/\sin^2 A(1-\sin B/B)}$ can be made arbitrarily small where **A** and **B** are angles and **R** is the radius of a sector. He depended on the works of **Clavius,** Valerio and Archimedes in proving his main proposition: the distance d between the center of a circle and the center of gravity of a circular sector can be given by the equation **3d = 2 R (chord A)/arc A.** He found this as preparation for the quadrature of the circle. Although this was the futile quest of so many at that time, it led to a beautiful set of theorems to be admired and used by many geometers to follow.

Bosmans also published some correspondence of **Gregory St. Vincent** in which he notes that while **de la Faille** was well-known as the tutor of Don Juan of Austria and died young in that capacity, he was a fine mathematician. Some appreciation of the above work is shown by Huygens who wrote to **St. Vincent**: "Your student (**de La Faille**) surpasses your colleague, **Paul Guldin**." In Christiaan Huygens' judgment **de la Faille** was a new Archimedes in his treatment of the center of gravity: "Archimedes invented this but **de la Faille** has mastered it."

When **de la Faille** died prematurely in Barcelona while on an expedition with Don Juan of Austria, **St Vincent** was greatly upset. Furthermore he wrote to Rome asking that the Spanish provincial send him **de la Faille**'s mathematical notes, because he felt that no geometers there in Spain would appreciate them and that they would simply get lost in the Spanish Jesuit archives. They were too valuable and his results were too beautiful not to be published. **Jean Charles de la Faille's** portrait by Anthony Van Dyke is found in a prominent place in the Plantin Museum *des Beaux Arts* in Brussels. (In l984 it was on loan to the Metropolitan museum in New York City.)

4. <u>Guldin's Rule</u>

Paul Guldin's second volume of *De centro gravitatis* contains what is known as **Guldin**'s rule: "If any plane figure revolves about an external axis in its plane, the volume of the solid so generated is equal to the product of the area of the figure and the distance traveled by the center of gravity of the figure."[35]

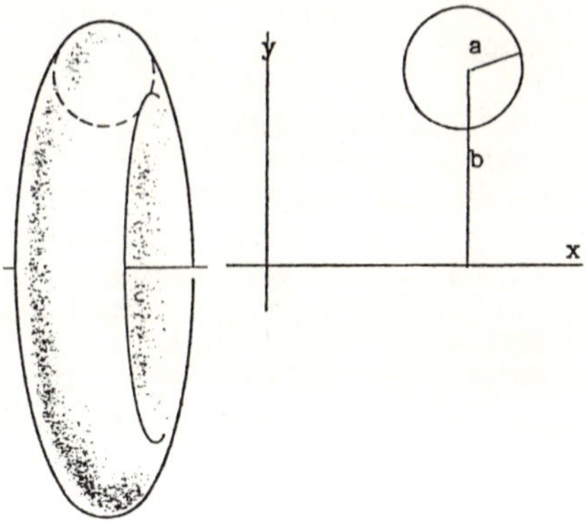

12 Guldin's rule:
Vol = 2π radius^2 x distance = $2Pa^2b$.
Modern texts recently have been calling this *Pappus'* rule.

Guldin did not know that the fundamental theorem which bears his name and which he used extensively, is found in a somewhat vague form in the *Collectio* of the well-known Greek mathematician Pappus (ca. A.D. 300). Nevertheless **Guldin** has been unjustly accused of plagiarism by earlier writers. This defamation has been removed, however, by recent historians expert in that period, such as Paul Ver Ecke, who shows that the translation of Pappus available to **Guldin,** and faithfully quoted by him, lacked the theorem in question.[36] Furthermore, he demonstrates that the accusation against Guldin is weakened by the fact that various geometers who lived at about the same time as **Guldin** did not credit Pappus with this theorem but **Guldin**. Among these writers is the noted astronomer Kepler, who presented applications of **Guldin's** theorem. The fact that Kepler failed to state **Guldin's** rule explicitly is explained by the custom of many of these early writers to give illustrative examples of a fundamental principle without stating it explicitly.

> The world owes a great debt of gratitude to those who, like Cardan and Guldin, contributed powerfully towards the enlightenment of the human race, especially at a time when so few people took an active interest in scientific matters. It seems therefore to be very fitting that wide currency should be extended to results which tend to remove from their names unjust defamatory associations due to carelessness on the part of earlier writers.[37]

In 1627 a correspondence on religious subjects developed between **Guldin** and Johannes Kepler when the latter wrote **Guldin** concerning his objections to the Catholic religion. **Guldin** tried to refute them with theological arguments, but apparently to no avail. Kepler had greater difficulties with Catholics than with the Catholic religion.

5. Other quadratures

Honoré Fabri contributed to understanding the quadrature of the cycloid in his geometrical works which Liebniz found so inspiring. Another Jesuit geometer **Antoine de la Louvere** is considered one of the precursors of modern integral calculus and was well known to the other mathematicians of the time. His most important work is the *Quadratura circuli* (1651), in which he finds volumes and centroids by inverting **Guldin's** rule. He moved from mathematics to theology until in 1658 he became embroiled in a dispute with Pascal over his solution for the problem of the "Roulette" (cycloid) posed by Pascal. Pascal's accusation that he plagiarized Roberval's solution was without foundation but the episode did bring **de la Louvere** back to geometry. **De la Louvere** found the solution to be what he called a "cyclocylindrique" (helix), described in his last work *Veterum geometria promota in septem de cycloide libris* (1660). Thus, **de la Louvere** became "the first mathematician to study the properties of the helix,"[38] according to W. W. Ball in his *History of Mathematics* (an author who expresses contempt for Jesuit efforts).

De la Louvere's chief book is the *Quadratura circuli* (1651), in which he drew upon the work of **de La Faille, Guldin**, and **St. Vincent**. His approach was an Archimedean summation of areas; he found the volumes and centers of gravity of bodies of rotation and curvilinearly defined wedges by indirect proofs. He was then able to proceed by inverting **Guldin's** rule whereby the volume of a body of rotation is equal to the product of the generating figure and the path of its center of gravity. Thus **de la Louvere** established the volume of the body of rotation and the center of gravity of its cross section; then by simple division he found the volume of the cross section. For this he is referred to as one of the precursors of the calculus. He later returned to theology, which he said was "an easier task more suited to my advanced age."

f. <u>Geometry as calculus evolved</u>

Unquestionably the most remarkable mathematical achievement of the 17th century was the invention of the calculus. This new tool proved to be astonishingly powerful in solving many problems that had been so baffling in earlier days. Much of this applicability lies in the field of geometry, and on the other hand a large part of geometry concerns properties of curves and surfaces which are examined by means of the calculus. Archimedes and Apollonius studied areas, volumes and normals of conic sections and later Cavalieri studied curvature and evolutes. But the first real stimulus to differential geometry was furnished by Gaspard Monge, a graduate of the Jesuit College de la Trinité in Lyons. He is considered the father of the differential geometry of curves and surfaces of space. Another differential geometer was **Boscovich** who was interested in developable surfaces (a kind of ruled surface) and osculating curves. Even though he contributed greatly to physics, he was more of a geometer than anything else.

> He preferred the geometric method of infinitely small magnitudes "which Newton almost always used" and which embodied the "power of geometry." He particularly applied it to differential geometry. . . In 1740 he studied the properties of osculatory circles and . . . in 1743 was the first to solve the problem of the body of greatest attraction.[39]

Today we treat the hyperbolic functions as pairs of exponential functions $(e^x \pm e^{-x})/2$ but their inventor, the Jesuit, **Vincent Riccati** (son of Jacob)[40] developed them and proved their consistency using only the geometry of the unit hyperbola $x^2-y^2 = 1$ **or** $2xy = 1$. **Riccati** followed his father's interests in differential equations which arose naturally from geometrical problems. This led him to a study of the rectification of the conics in Cartesian coordinates and to an interest in the areas under the unit hyperbola. **Riccati** developed the properties of the hyperbolic functions from purely geometrical considerations. He used geometrical motivation even though he was familiar with the work of Euler, who had introduced the symbol and concept of the natural number **e** and the function e^x ten years previous to **Riccati's** book. Lambert is sometimes given undue credit for these hyperbolic functions. **Riccati** had all the necessary details worked out and proven long before Lambert's treatise.[41]

Riccati's development of the hyperbolic functions may be described as follows. The algebra concerning circular sectors is simple since the arc length is proportional to the area of the sector. Hyperbolas, however, do not have this property, so a different algebra is needed. The latter arises naturally from a property peculiar to hyperbolas **xy = k** and evident in the figure. All right triangles **OAK** have the same area **k/2** no matter what point **A** is chosen on the curve. This property enables us to replace area measure by linear measure **OK**, thus introducing a kind of logarithm.

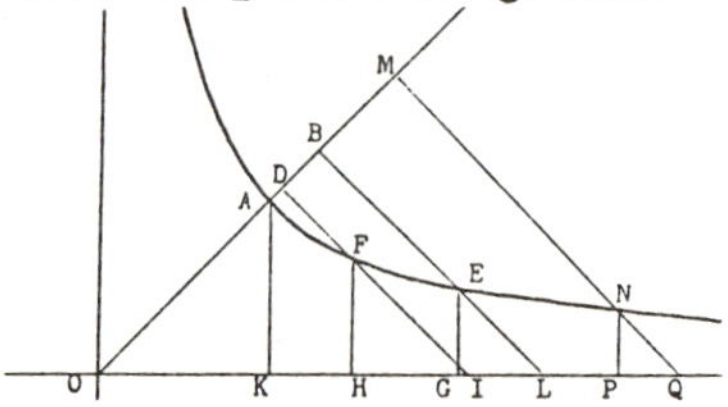

13 Vincent Riccati's logarithms for sinh and cosh functions
For all values of A triangles AOK have the same area since A lies on the hyperbola xy = k. Also areas AOK = FOH and so by addition AOF = AKHF. The other rules for these functions are motivated by using these and similar areas.

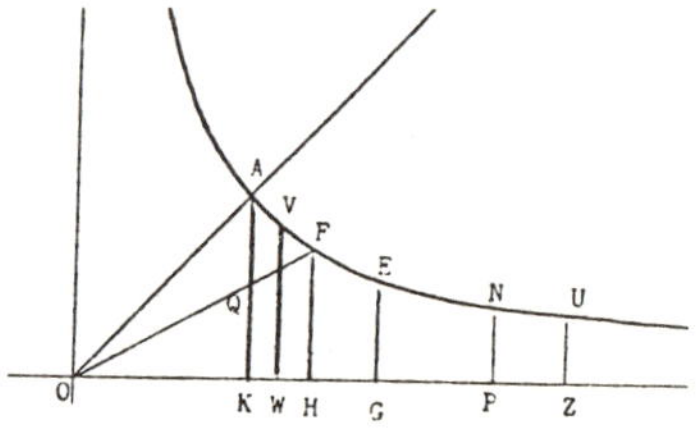

14 Derivation of identies for sinh and cosh functions are found by substituting multiplication of lengths for addition of areas: e.g. OKxOP = OGxOH since AKPN = AKHF + AKGE.

It can be seen from figures 13 and 14 that the following areas are equivalent: **AOK = FOH** because of the property just mentioned, **AOQ = QKHF** by subtracting the common area **OKQ**, **AKHF = AOF** by adding **AQF** to each. So for any point **F** on the curve, the area of the sector **AOF** equals the area under **AF.** This area function depends on point **F** as well as on **H**, the projection of **F** on the x-axis.

Addition and subtraction of areas can then be accomplished by multiplication and division of distances along the x-axis, and vice versa.

Given **G/K** = **P/H**, then
AKGE = ∫dx/2x
= .5 log(**G/K**) = .5 log (**P/H**)
= ∫dx/(2x) = **FHPN.**

Adding and subtracting then just involve constructing the correct proportions, i.e., finding the proper **OP** and **OG** for the proportions:

OK x OP = OG x OH which represents adding: **AKPN = AKHF + AKGE**
OG/OK = OP/OH which represents subtracting: **AKGE = AKPN - AKHF**

From these definitions of the hyperbolic functions and the logarithm operations, it is possible to derive a complete array of formulas regarding the double and triple arguments and from them to deduce other formulas for the square and cube roots. **Riccati** goes even further and proves the integral formulas for trigonometric as well as hyperbolic functions.[42]

Riccati and his collaborator Saladini present the first extensive treatise on integral calculus, predating that of Euler. This was an important step since they offered examples of integration as a result of direct additions of elements, instead of Newton's and Leibniz's concept

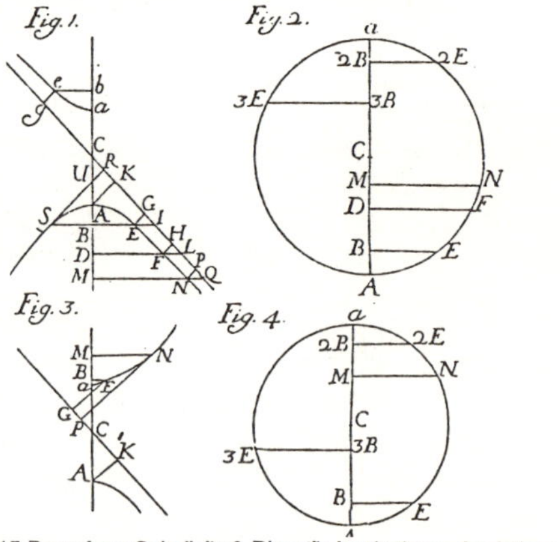

15 Page from Saladini's & Riccati's *Institutiones Analyticae* from Vol.I table 22,page 228,in which are proven the hyperbolic identities using purely geometrical arguments.

of integration as antidifferentiation.

Some other innovative works of **Riccati** include his treatment of the location of points that divide the tangents of a tractrix and also the problem posed by Guido Grandi about the four-leaf rose. Another Jesuit **Thomas Ceva** (brother of John)[44] investigated arithmetic-geometric-harmonic means. Also he contributed valuable insights into the cycloid as well as the higher conic sections.

Laplace gives credit to **Boscovich** for the method Laplace used to determine the most probable ellipse when he wrote, "**Boscovich** has given us for this purpose an ingenious method . . . in *Voyage Asronomique et Géographique.*" L.L.Whyte[45] describes the history of how the line of best fit was determined.

g. Non-Euclidean geometry

In 1621 Sir Henry Saville called attention to two blemishes ("naevi") in Euclidean geometry: the theory of parallels and the theory of proportion. The latter has already been mentioned concerning the works of **Christopher Clavius** in Chapter 2. As for the former, the fifth postulate was called the "scandal of geometry" by D'Alembert. But examination of this fifth postulate gave rise to new branches of geometry and showed that Euclid was freer from blemish than had been previously believed. The first step was to establish equivalent axioms. The parallel postulate, variously stated, is put most succinctly by Playfair: "Through a given point not on a given line can be drawn only one line parallel to the given line."

Clavius showed that this could be deduced from the fact that a line whose points are all equidistant from a straight line is itself straight. **Girolamo Saccheri** showed that it is sufficient to have a single triangle, the sum of whose angle are two right angles. Other equivalent forms do not show any essential superiority to Euclid's.

The attempts to derive the parallel postulate as a theorem from the remaining postulates of Euclid's Elements occupied geometers for over two thousand years and culminated in some of the most far-reaching developments of modern mathematics. Many "proofs" of the postulate were offered, but each was sooner or later shown to rest upon a tacit assumption equivalent to the postulate itself. Particularly outstanding was the 1733 work of **Saccheri** *Euclides ab omni naevo vindicatus,* "Euclid freed of every blemish," in which he tried to institute a *reductio ad absurdum* by finding a contradiction when the parallel postulate was denied. Though he failed in his efforts, he did bring to light a number of consequences that are recognized today as important theorems in non-Euclidean geometry.

Saccheri's work was an attempt (probably the first in print) to explain the principles of logic in a geometric sense. He was concerned about the definitions used by Euclid: the *nominal* definitions, which simply define a concept and the *real* definitions. These are nominal definitions to which a postulate of existence is attached. But this existence brings up the question whether one part of the definition is compatible with another part. In considering the parallelism between two lines he was the first to draw explicit attention to the question of compatibility between axioms. John Sullivan in "Mathematics as an Art" speaks in glowing terms of **Saccheri's** efforts.

Saccheri's attempt to demonstrate the parallel axiom was a miracle of ingenuity

> . . . Saccheri was an extremely able logician, too able to make an unjustified assumption. His method was to develop the consequences of denying the fifth axiom while retaining all the others. In this way he expected to develop a geometry that would be self-contradictory. He did not succeed in contradicting himself; what he did was lay the foundations for the first non-Euclidean geometry.[46]

Although **Clavius** early on brought attention to the troublesome fifth postulate of Euclid, it was not until **Saccheri** that a serious and concerted attempt was made to investigate its independence. **Saccheri** was one of the most accomplished of all Jesuit mathematicians and carried on extensive correspondence. Along with the Camaldolese monk Guido Grandi, for example, **Saccheri** wrote about quadratures and various curves. But he is best remembered for his contribution to non-Euclidean geometry.[47]

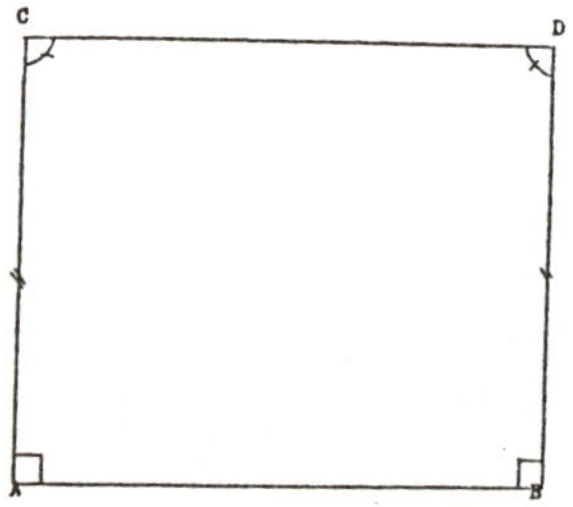

16 Saccheri quadrilateral showing trichotomy: (C+D) $< \pi$ or $= \pi$ or $> \pi$. His work stimulated later investigators to discover non-Euclidean geometry. Saccheri also proved many of the non-Euclidean theorems which are found in today's texts.

The distinguished Italian mathematician Eugenio Beltrami considered **Saccheri** the real founder of Non-Euclidean Geometry and brought it to other geometers' attention. Because of a subtle error **Saccheri** did not succeed in actually proving that the fifth postulate depends on the first four. Nonetheless, he states some of the most important theorems of non-Euclidean geometry known today, by making the assumptions that Gauss and Lobachevsky, who certainly had the works of **Saccheri** available to them, would make a century later. The great Gauss was to discover that the fifth postulate could be denied, but he found the new structure so shocking he was afraid to publish it.

Saccheri's work was forgotten for a century, until Beltrami published a note in 1889. Not only did **Saccheri** initiate a new approach to Euclid's fifth axiom but he proved many of the theorms that would have followed if the fifth postulate were replaced. Julian J. Coolidge has a thorough treatment of the background of non-Euclidean geometry.

> His note entitled "un precursore italiano di Legendre e di Lobachevsky" convinced the scientific world of the importance of Saccheri's work, and of the fact that theorems, which had been ascribed to Legendre, Lobachevsky and Bolyai had been discovered by Saccheri many years earlier.[48]

Much of **Saccheri's** book *Euclides* has been incorporated in the modern elementary treatment of the non-Euclidean geometries without sufficient credit. Instead, he is merely remembered for the error in his proof. **Saccheri** was convinced of the truth of the Euclidean hypothesis. His contradictory assumption was made to discover the contradiction which would follow, unlike Bolyai and

Lobachevsky, who wanted to prove the possibility of contradicting the fifth axiom.

His *Saccheri quadrilateral* is a two right-angled isosceles quadrilateral ABCD where A=B=90° and AC = BD. The C = D is not dificult to prove from the first 28 theorems (which do not depend on the fifth axiom). He discusses three possibilities. They are both right angles, they are both acute angles or they are both obtuse. These three possibilities as we know today refer to Euclidean, Lobachevskian or Reimannian geometries.

Boscovich 70 years later inherited the chair of **Saccheri** and realized the flaw in **Saccheri's** argument. **Boscovich** stated that the properties of parallels cannot be rigorously established by deduction from the rest of the axioms, so he knew that the fifth postulate could be replaced by another and a different definition of parallel line.[49] His thinking was not far from Gauss and Lobachevsky in anticipating non-Euclidean geometry.

h. Projective geometry

For centuries artists and architects sought formal laws of projection to place objects on a screen. **d'Aguilon's** *Opticorum libri sex* treated successfully projections and the errors in perception, and it was used by an architect Gérard Desargues,[50] who in 1639 published a remarkable treatise on the conic sections, emphasizing the idea of projection. But Desargues' work was so neglected by most other mathematicians of the time, because of his eccentric style and terminology, that it was soon forgotten. Most geometers then, spent their energies either developing the new powerful tool of analytic geometry or trying to apply infinitesimals to geometry.

In **d'Aguillon's** text on geometrical optics are found elements of perspectivities as well as the sterographic projections of Ptolemy and Hipparcus. He proposes experiments, drawn by Peter Paul Rubens, to study the variations of light intensity dependent on variations of distance. The Bouguer photometer can be traced to **d'Aguilon's** book.[51] More details of this work have already been covered in the first chapter.

Another projective geometer was **Honoré Fabri**, whose book on optics was used by Philip de la Hire. In this book **Fabri** states some of the principles of perspective geometry, and it is reviewed by the TRS.[52] The works of de la Hire were used in Peking by the Jesuit missionaries and by some of the Chinese painters in the 17th century, including Tshiao Ping-Chen who painted according to Western rules of perspective introduced by the Jesuits. The best 18th century Jesuit geometer in China was **Pierre Jartoux**, who also is credited with printing very accurate maps.

One of the most remarkable sights in Rome is the perspective painting on the ceiling of St. Ignatius Church done by the Jesuit brother **Andrea Pozzo**, a geometer-artist. He had been asked to come and decorate the church still under construction. On arrival he found that due to lack of funds no dome had been constructed. To fill this gap he took a flat piece of canvas and by his peculiarly brillant use of linear perspective created the illusion of a dome. By the sweep of his brush he gave St. Ignatius the giddy heights which the architect could not give. Then, on the flat, massive ceiling of the church he painted a fresco, in perspective, of the missionary spirit of Jesuit Society, thereby expressing Jesuit identification with the baroque spirit of Rome. He wrote a remarkable book on perspective geometry for artists and architects. *Prospettiva de' pittori ed architetti* (Rome, 1693-1700). Another Jesuit, Orazio Grassi, S.J. (d 1654), was the architect for the church, but it was **Pozzo** who started a new trend in Jesuit churches.

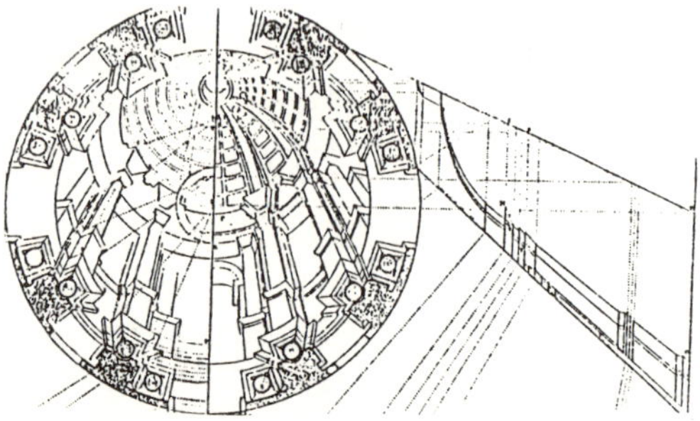

17 Andrea Pozzo's perspective drawing on a flat ceiling over the nave-transept at St Ignatius in Rome.

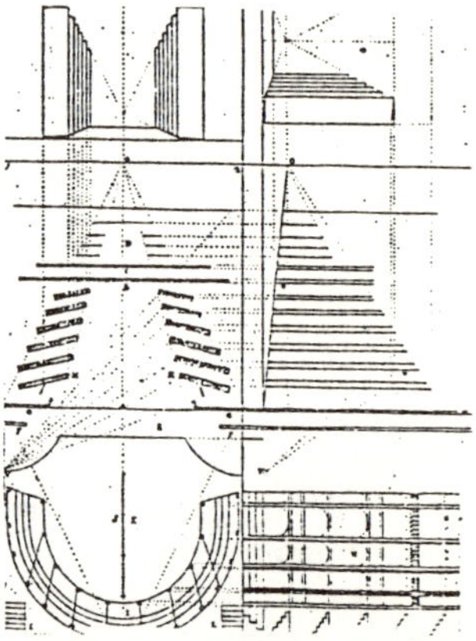

18 Andrea Pozzo's perspective drawing of his stage plan.

Several books have been written about **Pozzo's** contributions to *Jesuit iconography,* but he is best remembered as one of the most influential perspective theorists of the 17th century. His book on perspective transformations is in two volumes, has been reprinted many times and, originally written in Latin and Italian, has been translated into French, German, English,[53] Dutch and Chinese. It has been reissued as recently as 1971. In it he demonstrated how an irregular space could be represented on a stage by using wings obliquely. He emphasized the theoretical possibilities of perspective geometry and his works concerned one focal point (for example, two circles of red marble on the floor of St Ignatius Church are the focal points for viewing the ceiling). **Pozzo** expressed a new tendency in freer use of decorative elements in stage design. He tried to find a focal point of the perspective out of sight of the audience by displacing it to one side, thereby creating a more realistic effect. Three centuries later the cinema would put into practice some of his principles.

19 Brother Andrea Pozzo, S.J., who created the famous "cupola" on the flat ceiling of St Ignatius's church, as well as the magnificent soaring allegory of Jesuit missionary work. His book on perspective geometry has been reprinted for three centuries – the latest in 1971. Modern cinema has used some of his rules to achieve perspective.

> Pozzo alone had the opportunity to raise the whole structure in full scale; he did not hide the focus of the perspective at either side, out of view of the beholder. He could give an account of the gradual transition from real to reduced size on the stage without attaining the effect of a miniature world of the Mannerist stage. Thus he fulfills the legacy of the Jesuits Menghini and Rainaldi, which in turn is the most original and probably the most progressive aspect of the Jesuits' contribution to Baroque stage design.[54]

When critics accused **Pozzo** of misuse of the baroque style by resting the columns of his "cupola" on simple brackets, he replied wryly: "If my brackets give way and the columns start to fall to the ground, you will easily find some painters among my friends to remake them and remake them better." Over the years candle smoke had darkened his spurious dome, but recently this has been renovated by the Museums of Rome.

i. Geometry applied to physics

Newton experimented with the diffraction of light, but the discovery of this phenomenon was made by **Francesco Grimaldi,** professor of mathematics at the Jesuit college in Bologna. Furthermore, it was **Grimaldi** who named the phenomenon "diffraction" (breaking up). It was described in his work, *Physico mathesis de lumine* (1666). Through a small hole **Grimaldi** introduced a pencil of light into a dark room. The shadow cast by a rod held in the cone of light was allowed to fall upon a white surface. To his surprise he found the shadow wider than the computed geometrical shadow; moreover, it was bordered by one, two, and sometimes three coloured bands.[55]

Grimaldi was also the first to publish verification of Galileo's discovery for free-fall depending on the square of the time, and first to consider the effect on free-fall resulting from air resistance.

In the latter part of the l8th century **Roger Boscovich** was able to articulate an atomic theory using geometrical methods and in geometrical terms. The three principal ideas of his theory were that the ultimate elements of matter were points (atoms), which were centers of force and which force varied qualitatively and quantitatively in proportion to distance.

20 Verbiest's experiment: sun's ray illuminating the base of a cannon. He illustrated a lesson in geometrical optics realizing that the Emperor was quite partial to cannons.

His theory was so successful that his concepts of point centers were used (although **Boscovich** was not always quoted) by Priestly, Young, Faraday, Maxwell, Kelvin, Thompson, Gay-Lussac, Weber, Helmholz, Lorenz, and others.[56] As has already been mentioned, **Boscovich's** works have been collected and are kept in the Bancroft Rare Book Library at the University of California at Berkeley.

His influence in the history of atomic theory is seen from Maxwell's statement:

"The best thing we can do is get rid of rigid nucleus and substitute an atom of **Boscovich.**" And Kelvin, after experimenting with several axioms, concluded, "My present assumption is **Boscovichianism** pure and simple."[57]

Frequent articles in physics magazines center on his contribution to atomic physics l50 years before it was an acceptable theory. There were no fewer than five celebrations throughout the world on the bicentenary of his death in 1987, in Paris, Rome, Milan, Dubrovnik and Munich. These were held to commemorate the prophetic insights of **Boscovich**, who charted paths for the new science of atomic physics. His bold notion of "point-centers" abandoned the old concept of an assortment of different solid atoms. The fundamental particles of matter, he suggested, were all identical, and matter was the spatial relations around these point-centers. **Boscovich**, coming to these notions from mathematics and astronomy, foreshadowed the increasingly intimate connection between the structure of the atom and the structure of the universe, between the infinitesimal and the infinite.

Honoré Fabri is another who quickly applied the new calculus to the physical world and was the first to give a cogent reason for the experiment showing equal time for a body to fall.

Ignace Pardies in his *La Statique ou la science des forces mouvantes* (Paris, 1673) was interested in the tension in a flexible line and was responsible for the Pardies principle found in the solution of the suspension cable.[58] He argued that the form of a flexible line would remain unchanged if the forces at two points A and a were replaced by suitable forces acting along the tangents at A abd a. This princlple was used in the later work in analyses of the catenary by Bernouli and Leibniz.

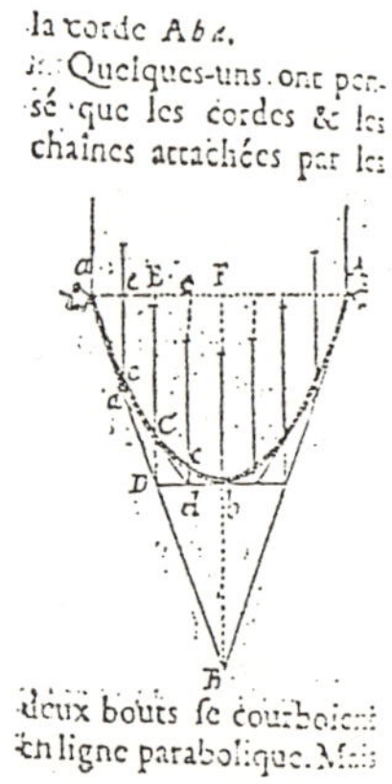

21 Part of Pardies' 1673 study of the suspension cable to solve the geometrical problem of tension in a flexible line.

Chapter 3 Footnotes

1. DSB, vol 3, p. 311-312.
2. Florian Cajori: *A History of mathematical notation*. Chicago: Open Court, 1928. Also see Jukutheil Ginsburg: "On the Early History of the Decimal Point." *American Mathematical Monthly*, vol 35 1928, p. 347-349. He states the case quite convincingly that Clavius, though ignored for centuries, was in fact the first to use the decimal point with full realization of what he was doing.
3. Christopher Clavius: *In Sphaeram Joannis de Sacrobosco*, 3rd. edition Venice: 1601, p. 13-15.
4. Charles Naux: "Le Père Christophore Clavius" in *Revue des questions scientifiques.* vol. 154, 1983 p. 335-336.
5. Z. Kopal:*Introduction to the Study of the Moon.* New York: Gordon & Breach,1966, p. 217
6. DSB, vol 11, p. 402-403.

7. William Bangert: *A History of the Society of Jesus.* St. Louis: Institute of Jesuit Sources, 1972, p. 160.
8. Rudolf Wittkower & Irma Jaffe: *Baroque art: the Jesuit contribution.* New York: Fordham, 1972, p. 68-88.
9. Carl Boyer: *History of mathematics.* New York: Wiley, 1968, p. 334.
10. DSB, vol 3, p. 312.
11. Christopher Clavius: *Astrolabium.* Rome: 1593, p. 178.
"Quaestiones omnes, quae per sinus, tangentes, atque secantes absolvi solent per solam prosthaphaeresim, id est, per solam additionem, subtractionemque sine laboriosa numerorum multiplicatione, divisioneque expedire."
12. D.E. Smith: *Source book in mathematics.* NewYork: McGraw-Hill, 1929, p. 455 and p. 459. Smith works from Jukutheil Ginsburg's translation of Clavius work.
13. Lancelot White: *Roger Joseph Boscovich*, New York:.Fordham, 1961, p. 41.
14. D. E. Smith: *History of Mathematics.* New York: Dover, 1958.
15. Florian Cajori: *A History of Mathematics.* New York: Chelsea, 1985, p. 181-182.
16. J. J. Coolidge: "The Origin of Polar Coordinates" in the *American Mathematical Monthly.* vol 59, 1952, p. 78-85. The author refers to Cantor's history.
Moritz Cantor: *Geschichte der Mathematik.* 2nd ed. Leipsig: vol. 2, 1900, p. 850.
17. Lancelot Whyte: *Roger Joseph Boscovich*, New York: Fordham, 1961, p. 184.
18. Ibid., p. 184-185.
19. Florian Cajori: *History of mathematics.* New York: Macmillan,1985, p. 262.
We conclude that Boscovich's influence was only mathematical in view of the author's story of Laplace's reply to the question "Why did you not mention the creator in your book *Méchanique Céleste*?" "Je n'avais pas besoin de cette hypothèse-la." ,
20. B. Sheynin, "Roger Boscovich's work on Probability", *Archives for History of Exact Sciences* vol. 9, 1973, p. 306-324.
21. Carl Boyer: *The concept of the calculus.* New York: p. 120-147.
22. D.J. Struik: *A concise history of mathematics.* New York: 1948, vol 2, p. 88.
23. DSB, vol. 9, p. 76.
24. George Sarton:*The Study of the History of Mathematics.* Cambridge: Harvard,1936, p.4.
25. J. M. Child: *The Early Manuscripts of Leibniz.* Chicago: Open Court, 1920, p. 14.
26. Florian Cajori: *History of mathematics.* New York: 1985, p. 181-182.
Also see DSB, vol. 12, p. 74-76..
27. Gregory St. Vincent: *Opus geometricum.* Antwerp: 1647, p. 55.
28. C. B. Boyer: *History of the Calculus.* New York: Columbia University Press, 1939, p. 136. He demonstrates how the "ductus" method works, illustrating that St. Vincent was considering infinitesimals in a completely new light.
29. James Newman: *The World of Mathematics.* New York: Simon & Schuster, 1956, vol. 1, p. 137.
30. Charles Naux: *Histoire des logarithmes.* Paris: 1871, p. 31. The author traces the logarithmic properties developed by Sarasa and St. Vincent.
31. DSB vol. 9 p. 75.
32. Carl Boyer: *History of The Calculus.* New York: Columbia, 1939, p. 55-57.
33. DSB, vol. 7, p. 558.
34 In *Mathesis*, vol. 41, 1927, p. 5-11.
35. Paul Guldin: *De Centro Gravitatis* . Vienna: 1635, chapter 7. prop. 3, p. 147.
36. DSB, vol. 5, p. 581.
Also see. Paul Ver Ecke, "Le Theorem dit de Guldin considéré au point de vu historique," *Mathesis.* 1932 vol. 46, 395-397. He shows that Guldin had access to an edition of the translation of Pappus' works which lacked this theorem.

37. *Science* vol. 64, #1652 8/27/26 p. 205.
38 W.W. Ball: *A Short account of the history of mathematics.* New York: 1901, p. 319 Also see DSB vol. 7, p. 583-584.
39. DSB, vol. 2, p. 330.
40. Angelo Fabronio: "De Tribus Riccatis" in *Vitae Italorum.* Pisa: Alexandrum Lande, vol. 16, 1795, p. 336-392. The author tells of the lives of the three Riccati mathematicians: the father, Count Jacobo and his two sons, Jordano and the Jesuit Vincentio. All three are buried together: "as they were joined in common study during life they could remain companions after death."
41. Moritz Cantor: *Vorlesungen uber Geschichte der Mathematik.* vol. 1, Leipsig: 1892, Teubner, p. 411.
Also Siegmund Gunther: *Die Lehre von den gewohnlichen und verallgemeinerten Hyperbelfunktionem.* Halle: Nebert, 1888, p. 1 - 55.
Also Florian Cajori: *A History of Mathematical Notation.* Chicago: Open Court,1928, p.172. Also, D. E. Smith: *History of Mathematics.* New York: Dover, 1958, p. 246-247.
42. Charles Naux: *Histoire des logarithmes.* Paris: 1871, p. 124- 149. This is a brief treatment of the main steps in Riccati's development of the hyperbolic functions. Also, see Joseph MacDonnell: "Using sinh and cosh to solve the cubic" in the *International Journal of Mathematical Education.* London: vol 18 #1 1987, p. 111-118.
43. DSB, vol. 7, p.402.
44. DSB, vol. 3, p. 183-184. Thomas was the brother of the geometer John after whom is named "Ceva's theorem." Guido Grandi corresponded with both brothers about cycloids.
45. Lancelot Whyte: *Roger Joseph Boscovich,* New York: Fordham, 1961, p. 200-210.
46. James Newman: *The World of Mathematics.* New York: Simon & Schuster, ed. 1956, vol. 3, p. 2019.
47. Henri Bosmans: "Le géometre Jerome Saccheri, S.J." in *Révue des questions scientifiques,* 4th ser., vol. 7, 1925, p. 401-430.
See also: Amedeo Agostini: "Due lettere inedite di Girolamo Saccheri" in *Memorie della Reale Accademia d'Italia* vol. 9, 9/28/30 p. 3-20. The author presents correspondence between Saccheri and Guido Grandi concerning the semicubical parabola.
48. Julian L Coolidge: *A History of Geometrical Methods.* London: Oxford, 1940, p. 12-13.
49. James Newman: op.cit., p. 187-189.
50. DSB, vol. 4, p. 48.
51. DSB, vol. 1, p. 181.
52. TRS, vol. 5, p. 2055.
53 Andrea Pozzo, S.J.: *Rules and examples of perspectives.* London: 1707. Reissued in New York: Benjamin Blom, 1971. This large (25 cm by 38cm) book has many perspective drawings of Pozzo as well as his rules for perspective drawing in both English and Latin.
54. Rudolf Wittkower & Irma Jaffe: *Baroque art: the Jesuit contribution.* New York: Fordham, 1972, p. 110.
55. Florian Cajori: *History of physics.* New York: Macmillan, 1898, p. 88.
56. Lancelot Whyte: *Roger Joseph Boscovich,* New York: Fordham, 1961, p. 121.
57. Ibid., p. 191.
58. Clifford Truesdell: *Essays on the history of mechanics.* New York: Springer-Verlag, 1968, p.20.

Chapter 4 Influence on Other Geometers

The influence Jesuits had on other geometers is treated under two headings:

a. In teaching other geometers
b. In correspondence with other geometers

a <u>In teaching other geometers</u>

Apart from the direct contributions to geometry, the Jesuits indirectly influenced its development by their relations with non-Jesuit geometers. They did this as teachers, as relatives, as friends, as correspondents, and as adversaries. Gilbert Highet speaks about the Jesuit educational experience in the years before the suppression of the Society.

> The best thing about its method was the thoroughness with which they planned. . . .The Jesuit regulations made sure that the pupils realized what they were doing, and why. It is noticeable that very many of their pupils have turned out to be men of very strong will-power and long vision. A good modern example is the Irishman who spent seven years on writing a book about the events of a single day, and then spent seventeen more on writing about the dreams of a single night. You may not admire *Ulysses* and *Finnegans Wake,* but they are monuments of aesthetic planning and perseverance, and it was the Jesuits who taught Joyce how to make such plans.
>
> The success of Jesuit education is proven by its graduates. It produced, first, a long list of wise and learned Jesuit preachers, writers, philosophers, and scientists. Yet if it had bred nothing but Jesuits it would be less important. Its value is that it proved the worth of its own principles by developing a large number of widely different men of vast talent: Corneille the tragedian, Descartes the philosopher and mathematician, Boussuet and Bourdaloue the orators, Moliere the comedian, d'Urfe the romantic novelist, Montesquieu the political philosopher, Voltaire the philosopher and critic, who although he is regarded by the Jesuits as a bad pupil is still not an unworthy representative of their ability to train gifted minds. The Company of Jesus had many enemies, but none of them ever said that it did not know how to teach. [1]

1 Gaspar Schott's publication of the Magdeburg experiment. Otto von Guericke asked Gaspar Schott, S.J. to describe his experiment of the exhausted hemispheres. He did so in *Guericke Experimenta* (1672), so that this famous dramatic picture on the cover of Schott's book has become a familiar sight to physics students for the past three centuries.

One of the well-known Jesuit teachers of geometers was Père Laurent Beraud,S.J. (1702-1777) who was born in Lyons, and taught mathematics in Avignon, Aix and Lyons, where he died. His obituary was printed in the *Journal des Scavans.* He taught two of the earliest historians of mathematics, Charles Bossut and Jean Etienne Montucla, as well as the distinguished astronomer Joseph Lalande. The latter received some of his formation in the special small college astronomy observatory constructed by Père Beraud. It was because of Beraud's encouragement that Bossut, whose mathematical preparation at the time was meager, dared to write to Bernard de Fontelle (another Jesuit alumnus), the secretary of the Académie Royale des Sciences, who introduced him to the famous mathematicians Clairaut and d'Alembert. This led to Bossut's interest in mathematics and to the history of mathematics. Later Bossut's treatment of the Society was certainly less than friendly, and he ended his days a devoted Jansenist. Despite this fact, he lists 16 Jesuits as the most important geometers of all time in a list of 303 names.

Some of the non-Jesuit geometer/scientists who were Jesuit-trained in one or other of the seven hundred Jesuit schools were Bossut, Jean Cassini, Descartes, Fontenelle, Ghetaldi, Guyton, Lagny, Lalande, Marci, Mersenne, Montucla, van Roomen, Torricelli, Valerio, Vivani, Volta, Zanotti. The contributions of these men to geometry as well as their relationship to the Society are all listed in the DSB. Below is a brief summary of their contributions and the names of the Jesuit schools they attended. This list, of course, does not include all geometers who were Jesuit educated.

2 Christopher Clavius, S.J. (1538-1612) was called Klaus, Claus, even Schluessel (key). He was also called "the greatest teacher of the Renaissance".

Jean Dominique Cassini(d 1712) was trained at the Jesuit college in Genoa. He introduced a class of curves, the Cassini ovals (of which the lemniscate is a special case). The ovals were first described in print by another mathematician, his son Jacques Cassini.

René Descartes (d1650) was one of the most celebrated Jesuit graduates and always had great praise for the Society. Of LaFlèche he said, "This is where was planted the first seeds of all my later accomplishments and for which I am eternally grateful to the Society of Jesus." He has been incorrectly listed by some historians as a Jesuit. He wasn't, of course, but he had a nephew Philip Descartes, S.J., who was a Jesuit mathematician. René Descartes was allowed to sleep late at LaFlèche because of ill health and later said that he found these morning hours the most productive of the day.

Bernard de Fontelle (d 1757), who attended the Jesuit school at Rouen, was secretary of the Académie Royale des Sciences. He later attacked the Jesuits because of what he considered their cavalier attitude toward miracles. Marino Ghetaldi (d 1626) was taught by **Christopher Clavius** and was a frequent correspondent of **Christopher Grienberger**. Louis Guyton (d 1816) had the Jesuits at Lyons, for which he was not terribly grateful. He wrote a poem satirizing the Jesuits and was rewarded by being chosen "honoraire" at the Académie des Sciences. After the suppression of the Jesuits, he proposed to the government a plan for dividing up and distributing the property of Jesuit schools.

Philippe de La Hire (d 1718) was taught by **Honoré Fabri** and later became part of a circle formed by **Honoré Fabri** which included Cassini, Deschales, both Huygenses, Leibniz, Descartes and Mersenne. La Hire was a pioneer in projective geometry and was considered by Carl Boyer in *A History of Mathematics* (New York, 1968) "the only mathematician of stature in France" after the demise of Desargues, Pascal and Fermat.[2]

Thomas Lagny (d 1660) attended the Jesuit college at Lyon. He was known for his theorems on convergence of series and with computational methods. Using one such series he computed π to 120 places. He also attempted to compose trigonometric tables using binary numbers.

Joseph LaLande (d 1807) also attended the college at Lyon and wanted to join the Jesuits but was unable to do so because of parental objections. He was one of the most prominent mathematician-astronomers of the century. It was his work that paved the way for the solution of the three body problem. He organized observations for two of those rare spectacular astronomical events, the transits of Venus across the sun in 1761 and 1769.

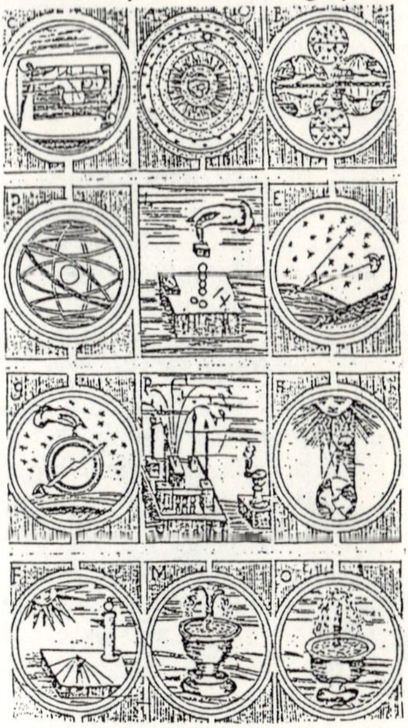

3 A page from the illustrated book of applied geometry by Pierre Bourdin,S.J. The readers learned twice; on each page a student found the lesson explained then illustrated.

Johannes Marci of Kronland (d 1667)[3] lived in Bohemia (now Czechoslovakia) and attended the Jesuit college in Jindrichuv Hradec. He was taught by **Gregory St. Vincent** at Prague and when in Rome met **Guldin** and **Kircher**. His work was mostly in geometrical optics but he was involved in physics and proposed using a pendulum clock for measuring pulse. During a political disturbance he initially represented the anti-Jesuit party at Prague University, but eventually the Jesuit school and the University of Prague joined together. On his deathbed he was admitted into the Jesuit Society.

Marin Mersenne (d 1648)[4] was trained by the Jesuits at La Flèche, and later became one of the most remarkable of all the Jesuit alumni. He became a Minim friar. In prejournal times he had the vision of developing a community of science. He lived in Place Royale (what is now Place des Vosges) in Paris, carrying on an intellectual apostolate. Not only Jesuit geometers would meet in his cell to discuss mathematics but also Gassendi, Descartes, Hobbes, Fermat, Pascal (in fact, if one were to look through the l2-volume work of his correspondence, one would find virtually all the geometers of his time).

Jean Montucla (d 1799)[5] was taught at the Jesuit college in Lyons and later wrote the first comprehensive and accurate description of the development of the various branches of mathematics in all countries. His friend Joseph LaLande completed Vol. III and IV after Montucla died.

Adriaan van Roomen (d 1615) attended the Jesuit school in Cologne. He knew **Clavius** and is remembered for his work on isoperimetric problems. His work *Ideae mathematicae pars prima* was dedicated to **Clavius.** In it he tried to find a general rule for calculating the sides of a polygon; he succeeded in finding to 32 decimal places the sides of polygons up to 15 **x** 2^{60} sides (by doubling sides) then with the help of one side of the regular 251,658,240 sided polygon he calculated π to 16 places.[6]

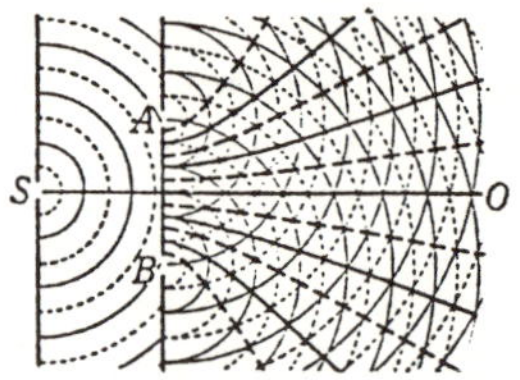

4 Diffraction ("splitting apart") was discovered and named by Francesco Maria Grimaldi, S.J. Isaac Newton learned of diffraction (which he called "inflection") by reading about it in the work of another Jesuit geometer Honoré Fabri. Grimaldi's terminology survived.

Evangelista Torricelli (d 1647)[7] attended the Jesuit school at Faenza. He wrote two letters to a former Jesuit teacher, Michael Ricci, S.J., in June 1644 to describe his successful experiment with a 76-cm column of mercury, which proved that vacuum exists.[8] The toys called "Cartesian devils" were invented by Torricelli, not by Descartes. His only book was *Opera geometrica* (1644), and he communicated to Mersenne his greatest discoveries, depending on Mersenne to relay them to other scientists. Even though he is remembered for his discoveries in physics, he spent all his life doing geometry. He had worked out twenty different ways to find the area of a parabola. He studied the generalized hyperbola $x^m y^n = c^n$ and thus anticipated the result of **Jean de la Faille** in 1632. In modern terms his process is an integral in Cartesian coordinates which is replaced by an integral in cylindrical coordinates. Cavalieri, Barrow and other pioneers of the calculus depended on the works of Torricelli.

Luca Valerio (d 1618) was taught by **Clavius** at the Roman College and influenced the thinking of Galileo.[9] Some of his geometry is found in Newton and Cavalieri (center of gravity), Torricelli, **de La Faille, Tacquet, St Vincent** and **Guldin.**

Vincenzo Viviani (d 1703)[10] attended the Jesuit school in Nente; he attempted to reconstruct the fifth book on conics of Apollonius. He duplicated the cube using conics and trisected the angle by using the cylindrical spiral or a cycloid and was also engaged in a number of other special geometrical problems.

The father of Alessandro Volta (d 1827)[11] had been a Jesuit for 11 years, his uncle was a Dominican and he himself was in a Jesuit seminary for a short time. Alessandro was the first to make quantitative measurements on the potentials of charged bodies and for him is named the unit of potential difference. He was a strong theoretician and some of his ideas on electricity were inspired by **Boscovich**.

Eustachio Zanotti (d 1782) was educated by the Jesuits in Bologna. He was a pioneer in the study of variable stars and proposed a lucid treatment of the method of indivisibles. His interest included perspectives and he contributed to the study of projections meant for artists as well as mathematicians.

A rather celebrated visitor to the Jesuit Roman College was Galilei Galileo. His friendship with members of the Society of Jesus started in 1587, when at the age of 23, he met **Christopher Clavius,** and continued for the rest of his life. Some incorrectly claim Galileo was a Jesuit; but in 1589 he did go away to become a monk, entering the monastery of Santa Maria in Vallombrosa as a novice, against his father's will, and within the year his father took him out of the monastery. Later in 1611 the Jesuits of the Roman College confirmed his discoveries of the motion of the earth and honored him, even though he had been embroiled in a dispute with **Scheiner** over a separate matter, the discovery of sunspots. Later he demolished **Scheiner's** idea that sunspots were tiny planets around the sun. In his writings he attributed his interest in falling bodies to a "certain Jesuit father, Niccolo Cabeo, S.J." Cabeo once described a type of wireless telegraph, with the admonition that it would be impossible to realize in practice.

The Dominican scholar William Wallace, O.P., in his book *Galileo's Early Notebooks* (Notre Dame, 1977), has demonstrated, by using the internal evidence of terminology, word order and symbols, that much of Galileo teachings came from Jesuits teaching at the Roman College. He names nine of them, thus corroborating the research of other scholars such as A. C. Crombie and Adriano Carigo. After studying Galileo's manuscripts for fifteen years, he found that all Galileo's notebooks show considerable evidence of copying. Practically all of the material derives from textbooks and lecture notes which were being used by the Jesuits at the Roman College. This evidence is available in collections like Sommervogel.

This was not considered plagiarism. People felt they had a right to ideas: when they were shown to be right, they were the property of everyone. In fact, teachers were flattered to have their class notes used by another instructor. Galileo is still the father of modern science, but now there is evidence that there was a grandfather as well. The grandfather which Wallace has been able to establish is a collection of nine Jesuit mathematicians and teachers of natural philosophy, such as **Christopher Clavius** and his colleagues: Benito Pereiro, Francisco de Toledo, Antonio Menu, Paul Valla, Muzio Vitelleschi, Robertus Jones, Stephanus del Bufalo and Ludovico Ruggiero. Though his Latin prose is more simple than **Clavius'** sophisticated style, the parallels between Galileo and **Clavius** are unmistakable. Galileo's debt to Jesuit contemporaries can be seen also in the authorities he quotes, who are identical to those quoted by the Jesuits.

Wallace itemizes the lecture notes in manuscript form that have been studied and identified as the same lecture notes which were used by Galileo:[12]

Benedictus Pererius, 1565-1566, *Physica, De caelo, De generatione*
Hieronymus de Gregoriis, 1567-1568, *Physica, De caelo, De generatione*
Antonius Menu, 1577-1579, *Physica, De caelo, De generatione*
Paulus Valla, 1588-1589, *De generatione*
Mutius Vitelleschi, !589-1590, *Physica, De caelo , De generatione*
Ludovicus Rugerius, 1590-1591, *Physica, De caelo ,De generatione*
Robertus Jones, 1592-1593, *Physica, De caelo*

Stephanus del Bufalo,1596-1597, *Physica, De generatione*

The mathematical organization was not new with Galileo, and the place of mathematics in physical analysis occurred to Galileo through contact once again with *reportationes* of the Collegio Romano. A mathematical approach to nature was indelibly etched in his Jesuit colleagues' physical mind-set by **Christopher Clavius**. It was **Clavius** who supplied the formal apparatus for "geometrical philosophy," and his influence on Galileo through his commentary on Sacrobosco was apparent. **Clavius** knew all the techniques of handling motion which had been invented since the fourteenth century. In other words, the Roman Jesuits were the immediate source of a number of Galileo's leading mathematical concepts. The notion of specific gravity ultimately descends from Archimedes, but it was made proximately available to Galileo through lecture notes, for example, those of Valla, Vitelleschi, and Rugerius. Examples of the evidence include Galileo's phrasing identical with that of the Jesuits' as well as of authorities cited: Ockham, Sylvester of Ferrar, Durandus, St. Thomas and Scotus. In his review of Wallace's book these things were mentioned by William Shea, who points out that the professors of the Roman College frequently made their notes available to their students.

> Wallace argues that lecture notes of four other Jesuit professors show even more striking parallels and coincidences with the words actually used by Galileo. . . Wallace has given us an outstandingly lucid and intelligent account of matters of great interest. This book is the first comprehensive and unified treatment of the influence that the Jesuits exerted on one of the greatest minds of all times.[13]

b <u>In correspondence among geometers</u>

Hooke performed his first experiments on diffraction after reading of **Grimaldi's** book in the Philosophical Transactions of the Royal Society. Furthermore both Hooke and Newton show familiarity with his works.[14] Newton credits **Fabri** as the source of his knowledge on diffraction. Newton's initial description shows he did not perform the experiments outlined by **Grimaldi.** Later when Newton did perform the experiments, he referred to it as a kind of refraction and by careful measurements made clear the periodic nature of the phenomenon.

5 Jean Charles de la Faille, S.J. (1597-1654) sketched from the painting by the artist Anthony Van Dyke. The painting was once on display in New York and is now hanging in the Plantin Museum of Fine Art in Bruxelles.

As has been suggested, many of the geometers at this time, though not trained by Jesuits, were familiar with their books. Leibniz was inspired and enlightened by them, as were Huygens, Barrow, Desargues, Gregory, Lambert, Mercator, Boyle, and Newton, by their own admission.

There were many strong friendships between Jesuit and non-Jesuit geometers. The son-in-law of Tycho Brahe once told **Clavius** that he should write more often to Tycho and that he should not hesitate to ask for anything, because even though Tycho Brahe was not Catholic he was not a bigot, and in fact liked **Clavius.**[15] Another instance of strong friendships is the fact that it was to the Jesuits that Galileo turned during his crisis with the Church. In 1588 this unknown young scientist wrote to **Clavius** asking about a center-of-gravity demonstration and expressed great admiration for **Clavius**. From the remarks in this letter, as well as in later letters, his esteem for Jesuits is quite compelling.

> I prefer Your Reverend Lordship's (Clavius) judgment above that of any other. If you are silent, I shall be silent, too: if not, I shall turn to another demonstration. . . . I know that with friends of truth like Your Reverend Lordship one may and ought to speak freely. Excuse my delight in dealing with you, and continue to grant me your grace, for which I supplicate you in every instance. Also gain for me the grace of the other, Father Christopher (Grienberger), your disciple, whose reputation for mathematical ability has aroused my highest admiration.[16]

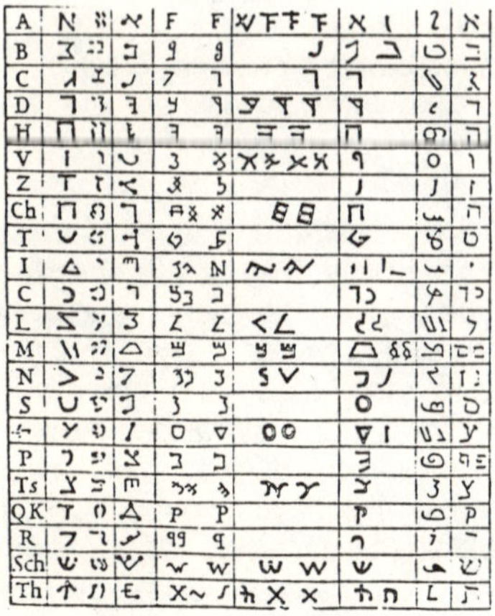

6 Kircher's *tabula combinatoria*, comparing the known alphabets. Kircher is called the "founder of Egyptology".

When Galileo, with the help of his "cannocchiale" or "telescopio" discovered the phases of Venus, the "three-bodied" appearance of Saturn, and the mountains of the moon, **Clavius** verified these phenomena and praised Galileo for his discoveries. Galileo was delighted and expressed his joy with Clavius' compliments, "as much appreciated as it was desired and little expected," bringing him "such testimony to the truth" of his observations. In fact Galileo was sick in bed when he received Clavius' letter and claimed that the letter brought him so much joy, it occasioned his immediate recovery. Galileo knew the impact **Clavius**' opinions had on the learned world, and wrote: "All the experts, especially the Jesuit fathers, agree with me, as everybody will soon know."

There was a voluminous and constant flow of correspondence between Jesuit and non-Jesuit geometers of these two centuries. In Rigaud's *Correspondence of Scientific Men of the Seventeenth Century*[17] Jesuit names frequently appear. Letters passed, for instance, between Galileo, Viete, both Cassinis, both Huygens, Fermat, Descartes, Leibniz, Newton and Kepler and many Jesuit geometers such as **Clavius, Scheiner, Guldin, de la Faille, de Chales, Grienberger**. In Mersenne's twelve-volume collection of correspondence are found many Jesuit entries.

The works of Joannes Kepler have been collected into 18 huge volumes and published by Max Caspar. Among the curious items is one concerning Thomas Lydiat, the rector of Oxford, who, with obvious scorn, called Kepler's chronology of the life of Jesus Christ "that of the Jesuits." Kepler, smarting from the intended insult, wrote a criticism of Lydiat's book. "Judging by the way Jesuits are treated in England, it must be a great crime to hold Jesuit doctrine; but if Lydiat has no more serious charge against the Jesuits than that they approve the Keplerian chronology, by that very charge the conduct of his country stands condemned."

Kepler had a long friendship with Jesuits, even though he found himself in controversy with them frequently.[18] **Guldin** was quite devoted to Kepler's studies and well-being. An edict had been issued that all non-Catholics had to move out of Linz; so when Kepler refused to capitulate and become a Catholic, he was exiled from Linz and had to move to Graz and so was cut off from Prague. In 1626 he had been thinking about becoming a Catholic, but the more he learned of Catholics the less inclined he was to become one.

Quadratum opticè delineatum.

POSTQUAM *deſcripſeris in papyro ſeparata qnadratum geometricum* A, *facies duas lineas parallelas inter ſe diſtantes altitudine, quam dederis puncto oculi; linea inferior erit linea plani, linea ſuperior erit linea horizontalis, ſuper quam ponuntur puncta oculi* O, *& diſtantiæ* E, *quod ſit ex parte quam mavis: linea diſtantiæ non debet eſſe brevior magnitudine rerum deſcribendarum. Transfer poſteà circino latitudinem quadrati* A *in* CB, *unà cum viſualibus ad punctum* O; *& ſimiliter transfer longitudinem ipſius quadrati in* DC, *ducens lineam à puncto* D *ad punctum diſtantiæ* E, *tranſeuntem per viſualem* CO, *& ubi illa ſecat, habebis terminum quadrati optici* GFCB, *ducens parallelam ad lineam plani in* F.

7 One of Andrea Pozzo's rules for perspective drawing from his book *Perspectiva pictorum,* which has gone through many editions and was widely circulated.

Guldin was concerned about Kepler's financial predicament as well as his inability to study the skies, since he owned no telescope. The Jesuit **Nicolas Zucchi** was well known as a telescope maker; at the urging of **Guldin,** he brought a telescope to Kepler. Kepler, like a child with a new toy, wrote to **Guldin** of his gratitude for the latter's concern and kindness. It was one of many letters he would write to **Guldin** in his lifetime and these are published in the *Johannes Kepler Gesammelte Werke.*[19] One of the most touching letters was the dedication of his last book, *The Dream by Johannes Kepler, the late imperial mathematician, a posthumous work on lunar astronomy* (1634), published by his son after he died. In this work he tells of his discoveries concerning the surface of the moon and describes an imagined trip there as well as how it might be inhabited. At the end of the book he publishes a long letter of gratitude which he sent to Guldin. In part it reads:

> Geographical, or, if you prefer, Selenographical Appendix.
> To the very reverend Father Paul Guldin, priest of the Society of Jesus, venerable and learned man, beloved patron. There is hardly anyone at this time with whom I would rather discuss matters of astronomy than with you . . . Even more of a pleasure to me, therefore, was the greeting from your reverence which was delivered to me by members of your order who are here . . . think you should receive from me the first literary fruit of the joy that I have gained from trial of this gift (the telescope).[20]

The Jesuits in China had much more success in dealing with Kepler than with

Galileo as they attempted to keep abreast of astronomical developments. The Protestant Kepler wrote often in response to Jesuit Jean Schreck's (**Terentius**) requests for information, and at the end of one letter expresses an ecumenical prayer for the conversion of the Chinese.

> Quod ratum esse velit Is cui Pater aeternus gentes in haereditatem dedit, Christus Iesus, Deus et homo, Dominusque noster. Amen. ("May Jesus Christ, God and man, and our Lord, to Whom the Eternal Father gave the heathen as an inheritance, will it (the conversion of the Chinese) to be fulfilled. Amen.") [21]

Although unpleasant at times, the many controversies Jesuit geometers engaged in did not end without some profit for geometry and science. In a long and bitter dispute with Kepler **Scheiner** forced Kepler to a more precise formulation of his terms. **Scheiner** used the pseudonym "Appelles", taken from the Greek myth. No one could draw a line finer than the artist Appelles. Similarly Cavalieri became more careful when his ideas were criticized by **Guldin.** Cavalieri as well as the geometer Stefano Angeli (d 1623), were Jesuati (Gesuati), the order of St. Jerome adhering to the Augustinian rule, which was suppressed by Clement IX in 1668. They both are sometimes incorrectly referred to as Jesuits. Angeli was involved with **Guldin** and **Tacquet** in a dispute over indivisibles. **Jean de la Faille** had wide correspondence with Christian Huygens and Langren. Henri Bosmans published a number of letters between Christian Huygens and **André Tacquet** in which reference is made to correspondence with many other geometers of the day.[22]

A frequent correspondent of **Jacques de Billy** was Pierre de Fermat; this affected the work of both geometers. Fermat has been referred to as "the prince of amateur mathematicians" and has been called by Laplace "the true inventor of the differential calculus."[23] He was a devout Catholic; his son Jean was an archdeacon and his daughters Catherine and Louise were religious nuns.[24] Fermat is best remembered for "Fermat's Last Theorem": $x^n + y^n = z^n$ never holds for integers x,y,z and n if n>2. This has been one of the most notorious unsolved problems for the past 350 years. To make matters worse, Fermat claimed that he had a remarkable proof, but that it would not fit into the margins. Some have not been very gracious at being unable to find a proof and have consoled themselves that the proof would not be useful anyway. The fact that $3^2 + 4^2 = 5^2$ was used to construct right angles for the pyramids but of what value are the higher orders? even the special triple case of $3^3 + 4^3 + 5^3 = 6^3$? There are, moreover, two questions: Did Fermat really have a proof? and what was his proof?

When Pascal tried to take credit for Torricelli's experiments, Jesuit geometers corrected him; after that Pascal had a stormy relationship with the Jesuits. He found himself in bitter arguments more than once. One example is his claim that **Antoine de la Louvere** did not really solve a problem concerning the roulette. Pascal lost this battle but won more contests with the Jesuits than he lost. D'Alembert, the angry encyclopedist, in spite of his hatred for the Jesuits, came to **Roger Boscovich** for help when he was deprived of a mathematics chair which he felt he deserved. The chair had been left vacant on the death of Clairaut and d'Alembert was told that his field of mathematics was not suitable. In desperation, in a frantic letter written in haste and filled with grammatical errors, he begs **Boscovich** to help him. A translation of a few lines of this letter follows:

> I ask you reverend Father, for the love which you have for me, to take this news to all the intellectuals of Italy who hold me in esteem.[25]

Ignace Pardies made his most important scientific contribution, not in his writings, but in his correspondence. It is there that we find the objections that **Pardies** expressed to Newton concerning his theory of colors and the "experimentum crucis" - objections that enabled Newton to clarify certain difficult points.[26] **Pardies** was a temperate and courteous critic of Newton.[27] He was a vigorous intellect, as is evident from his pedagogical writings and his contacts with the pioneers of geometry. Leibniz' impression of him confirms this view.

After meeting in Rome with the Jesuits on their way to the Chinese mission, Leibniz started a correspondence with them and sent a suggestion for explaining the Holy Spirit as part of a Trinity to the mathematically minded Chinese. He suggested using the analog to the square root of minus one as sort of intersection of number and non-number. Leibniz was inspired by the work of **Kircher** to attempt to find an alphabet of thought which would enable all to speak of the creation of knowledge. Leibniz also wrote to Bernoulli in 1703, attributing his original interest in mathematics to the writings of Jesuit geometers.

> As a child, I had studied the elementary algebra of one Lancius, and later that of Clavius; as for that of Descartes, it struck me as being too difficult. I asked Buot for the work of Dettonville and of Gregory de St. Vincent, which was kept in the Royal Library. Without delay, I studied these works - these gems invented by St. Vincent and perfected by Pascal. I culled everything that I could derive from the work of Cavalieri, Guldin, Torricelli, Gregory de St. Vincent, and Pascal on sums of sums and transpositions. [28]

Gaspar Schott added as an appendix to his *Mechanica Hydraulio-pneumatica* (1657) a detailed account of Guericke's experiments on vacuums, the earliest published report of this work. As a result he became the center of correspondence, as other geometers wrote to inform him of their inventions and discoveries. **Schott** exchanged several letters with Guericke, seeking to draw him out by suggesting new problems, and then published his later investigations. He also corresponded with Huygens and was the first to make Boyle's investigations on the air pump widely known in Germany. Even though he personally held the Aristotelian abhorrence of a vacuum, he was open to new information from experiments and rendered great service to Germany by encouraging experimentation. Like Mersenne, he spread news of new investigations, observations and discoveries; he suggested fresh problems and encouraged controversies until there was a resolution. It was his publication of von Guericke's research that stimulated Robert Boyle to have an airpump constructed.[29]

Chapter 4 Footnotes

1. Gilbert Highet: *The Art of teaching.* New York: Knopf, 1954, p. 221 and p. 224.
2. Carl Boyer: *A History of mathematics*. New York: Wiley, 1968, p. 404.
3. DSB vol. 9, p. 96-97.

4. DSB vol. 9, p. 316.
5. DSB vol. 9, p. 500.
6. DSB vol. 11, p. 532-533.
7. DSB vol. 13, p. 433.
8. DSB vol. 9, p. 332.
9. DSB vol. 9, p. 561.
10. DSB vol. 14, p. 48.
11. DSB vol. 14, p. 69.
12. William A. Wallace: *Galileo's early notebooks.* Notre Dame: Notre Dame, 1977, p.13. A very useful source for this work is the book review by John Quinn, O.S.A, "The scholastic mind of Galileo: the Jesuit connection" in the *International Philosophical Quarterly*, vol. 20 #3, 1980, p. 347-362.
13 William Shea: "Readings of Galileo" in *Science* vol. 227, Mar 22, 1985. p.1462-1463.
14. DSB vol. 5, p. 544.
15. Edward Phillips: "Correspondence of Father Christopher Clavius" in *AHSI* vol. 8 1939, p. 193-222. Phillips lists 291 letters to Clavius from geometers as well as church and civil potentates.
Also see: Francisco Sanches: "Ad C. Clauium epistola" in *Opera Philosophic Coimbra*, 1955 p. 146-153.
16 Pasquale M. D' Elia, S.J.: *Galileo in China.* Cambridge: Harvard Univeristy,1960, p. 7-9 D' Elia gives the references to these letters of Galileo taken from the Archives of the Pontifical Gregorian University.
17 S. J. Riguard, ed.: *Correspondence of Scientific Men of the Seventeenth Century.* 2 vols. London: Oxford University Press, 1841.
Also see: A. de Morgan: *Contents of the Correspondence of the 17th and 18th century.* London: Oxford, 1862.
18. M. W. Burke-Geffney:*Kepler and the Jesuits.* Milwaukee: Bruce, 1944, p. 130.
19. Max Caspar: *Johannes Kepler Gesammelte Werke.* 18 vols. Muenchen: C. H. Becksche, p. 195.
20. Johannes Kepler: *The Dream of Kepler.* Silesia: 1634, p. 165.
21. Pasquale M. D' Elia, S.J.: *Galileo in China.* Cambridge: Harvard University, 1960, p. 33. D' Elia quotes from Schreck's letter and the reply in *Kepleri Opera Omnia*, VII, p. 667-681.
22. Henri Bosmans: "Le Jesuite Mathématicien Anversois André Tacquet" in *Gulden Passer.* vol 3, 1925, p. 63-87.
23. Carl Boyer: *History of Mathematics.* New York: Wiley, 1968, p. 367.
24. DSB vol. 2, p. 131. Both carried on an active correspondence which precipitated some of de Billy's writings: for example, his treatment of indeterminate analysis was shared by Fermat.
25. G. Arrighi: "J L D'Alembert, R G Boscovich ed un Patrizio Lucchese" in *Bollettino Storico Lucchese,* vol. 2 1930, n. 3, p. 27-248 ". . . Je vous prie, mon Rérérend Père, par l'amitié que vous avez pour moi, de vouloir bien apprendre cette nouvelle a tous les Savans d'Italie, qui m'honnorent de leur estime."
26. DSB vol. 10, p. 315.
27. James Newman: *The World of Mathematics.* New York: Simon & Schuster, ed. 1956, vol. 1, p. 260.
28. René Tatan: *Beginning of Modern Science*: Pomerans, 1958, p. 228-229.
Also see: Joseph E. Hofmann: *Das Opus geometricum des Gregorius a S Vincentio und seine Einwirkung auf Leibnitz.* Berlin: 1942.
29. DSB vol. 12, p. 210.

Chapter 5 Innovations in Teaching Geometry

Jesuit geometers made their greatest contribution in their teaching. Many of their books were meant as classroom texts. In their schools they insisted that all students learn geometry and that geometry be taught properly. Evidence of how serious they were is taken from four sources:

a. Their insistence that geometry be in the curriculum
b. Their innovative attempts to teach geometry clearly and with enthusiasm
c. Their interventions stimulating others to clarify concepts
d. Their efforts to disseminate current geometrical discoveries

a. Their insistence that geometry be in the curriculum

Because of remarkable successes in the early years, the Society of Jesus was asked to open many schools throughout Europe, and the norms for granting degrees as well as the types of subjects to be taught varied from place to place. It was evident that some standard process was needed. After years of discussion and experimentation, a committee which included **Christopher Clavius** completed the third version of a proposed plan, called the *Ratio Studiorum*. This was promulgated in 1599 by the Jesuit General, Acquaviva. Geometry would be a regular part of the curriculum in Jesuit schools, and Jesuit scholastics would take mathematics while they were studying philosophy. While individual schools already taught geometry, this third version marked the first time a geometry requirement for all students was made by the whole Jesuit educational system.

In later years many superiors, Robert Bellarmine among them, wrote letters urging care in the teaching of mathematics and the training of mathematics teachers. In his time **Clavius** had these observations to make about the training of mathematics teachers and the formation of a mathematics society 350 years before the birth of the American Mathematical Society.

> To the end that mathematical studies be held in higher esteem . . . the mathematics teacher should be invited to disputations. Many a professor of philosophy has made no end of mistakes because of his ignorance of mathematics. Once a month scholastics [Jesuit seminarians] should be gathered . . . to hear original demonstrations of the propositions of Euclid.
>
> However, that the Society may be able always to have capable teachers of mathematics, a number of men fit and able to undertake such positions ought to be chosen and organized in a *private academy* for the study of the branches of mathematics. Otherwise it doesn't seem possible for these studies to survive, much less advance, in the Society.
>
> It was proposed last year that, for the advancement of mathematical studies (which were being almost neglected), those who were to teach mathematics should be excused from teaching grammar, that they might, during the first year after finishing philosophy, study mathematics more thoroughly at home, and then teach

publicly one or two years. This plan was approved, and has even to some extent been put in practice, and promised to be of the greatest use in encouraging mathematics and also in promoting the full equipment in other studies.[1]

A special school for mathematics was started in 1611 at Antwerp by **François d'Aguilon** and produced Jesuit geometers such as **Tacquet** and **de la Faille**. It demonstrated how serious the Society was about geometry. The French Jesuits also developed an important mathematical school which flourished for generations, and Jean Baptiste Colbert, minister of Louis XIV, entrusted to the Jesuits the teaching of hydrography in the French navy.

b. <u>Their innovative attempts to teach geometry clearly and with enthusiasm</u>

Clavius' widely used textbook *Geometrica practica* (1604) illustrated the concern that geometry be treated not merely as a spatial exercise but with rigor. This was emphasized many times later by subsequent authors and commentaries on Euclid. One work emphasizing the need to take care in the presentation of the matter was *Cursus seu mundus mathematicus* (Lyons, 1674) by **Claude F. M. de Chales**. In it **de Chales** urged that all Euclid's books not be treated equally, since some parts are more important and more intelligible for the beginner than others. His book is reviewed in the Philosophical Transactions of the Royal Society: their review of *Mundus mathematicus* praised the teaching principles of this geometry book.

Concerning Euclid, he dissuades from teaching novices all the books of Euclid indifferently; alleging to have learned by experience that, at the beginning, time is ill spent in learning his 7th, 8th, 9th and 10th Books[2]

Another such was work was *Elementa geometriae* (1654) of **André Tacquet** which so influenced Roberval, Pascal and Fermat. His book went through many editions and was distinguished for its clarity and order. For this reason it was used for generations of readers and was called by Henry Oldenburg, the founder of the TRS, "one of the best books ever written in Mathematics."[3] He comments further: ". . . being an account of one of the most considerable volumes of mathematics extant, we hope we may be the better excused for its prolixity."[4] **Honoré Fabri** tried to unify all physics along the lines of geometry; as it was described in the TRS, "Concerning his method he hath comprehended the whole of Physics in a geometrical method."[5] It was **Honoré Fabri** who first explained Galileo's experiment demonstrating equal time for falling

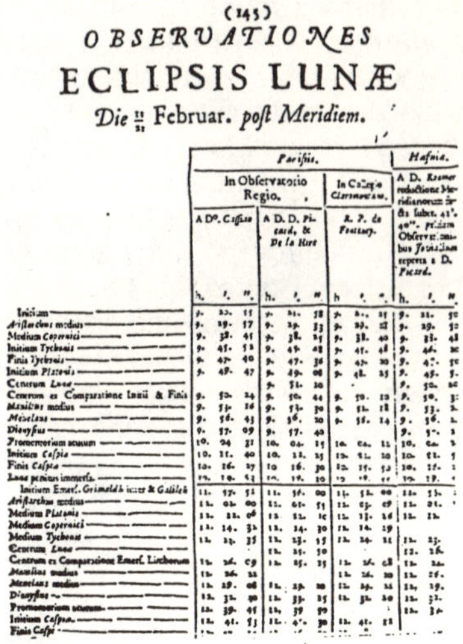
(145)
OBSERVATIONES
ECLIPSIS LUNÆ
Die 11/21 Februar. *post Meridiem.*

	Parisiis.												Hafniæ.		
	In Observatorio Regio.						In Collegio Claromontano.						A D. Roemer reductione Meridianorum facta subtr. 41'. 40". primæ Observationibus Parisiensibus repertæ a D. Picard.		
	A D°. Cassino			A D. D. Picard, & De la Hire			R. P. de Fontaney.								
	h.	'.	".	h.	'.	".	h.	'.	".				h.	'.	".

	h.	'.	".	h.	'.	".	h.	'.	".	h.	'.	".
Initium	9.	22.	55	9.	21.	58	9.	[illegible]	25	9.	21.	5[illegible]
Aristarchus medius	9.	29.	17	9.	29.	33	9.	29.	28	9.	29.	[illegible]
Medium Copernici	9.	38.	45	9.	38.	25	9.	38.	40	9.	38.	48
Initium Tychonis	9.	45.	52	9.	45.	48	9.	45.	48	9.	46.	[illegible]
Finis Tychonis	9.	47.	40	9.	47.	36	9.	47.	30	9.	47.	[illegible]
Initium Platonis	9.	49.	47	9.	49.	08	9.	48.	35	9.	45.	[illegible]
Centrum Lunæ				9.	51.	10				9.	50.	[illegible]
Centrum ex Comparatione Initii & Finis	9.	50.	24	9.	50.	44	9.	50.	10	9.	50.	[illegible]
Manilius medius	9.	53.	16	9.	53.	30	9.	52.	18	9.	53.	[illegible]
Menelaus	9.	56.	45	9.	56.	20	9.	55.	14	9.	56.	[illegible]
Dionysius	9.	57.	09	9.	57.	40				9.	57.	[illegible]
Promontorium acutum	10.	[illegible]	31	10.	04.	15	10.	02.	12	10.	02.	[illegible]
Initium Caspiæ	10.	11.	40	10.	12.	25	10.	11.	20	10.	11.	[illegible]
Finis Caspiæ	10.	16.	27	10.	16.	30	10.	15.	52	10.	15.	[illegible]
Luna penitus immersa	[illegible]	19.	53	10.	19.	20	[illegible]	[illegible]	[illegible]	[illegible]	19.	[illegible]
Initium Emers. Grimaldi inter & Galilei	11.	57.	51	11.	56.	00	11.	52.	00	11.	55.	[illegible]
Aristarchus medius	12.	02.	00	12.	01.	55	12.	03.	09	12.	01.	[illegible]
Medium Platonis	12.	12.	06	12.	12.	16	12.	13.	16	12.	12.	
Medium Copernici	12.	14.	32	12.	14.	30	12.	14.	19			
Medium Tychonis	12.	23.	35	12.	23.	55	12.	24.	22	12.	23.	
Centrum Lunæ				12.	25.	50				12.	26.	
Centrum ex Comparatione Emers. Limborum	12.	26.	09	12.	25.	25	12.	26.	08	12.	[illegible]	
Manilius medius	12.	26.	22				12.	26.	30	12.	26.	
Menelaus medius	12.	29.	08	12.	29.	30	12.	29.	22	12.	29.	
Dionysius	12.	32.	40	12.	33.	25	12.	32.	40	12.	32.	
Promontorium acutum	12.	39.	45	12.	39.	50				12.	39.	
Initium Caspiæ	12.	41.	53	12.	[illegible]	30	12.	41.	22			
Finis Caspiæ	[illegible]	[illegible]	[illegible]	[illegible]	[illegible]	[illegible]	[illegible]	[illegible]	[illegible]	[illegible]	[illegible]	

1 Report of Jean Fontanoy, S.J.: observations of eclipses printed in the Transactions of the Royal Society

bodies.
Galileo, in turn, had gotten interested in the problem in the first place because of the writings of another Jesuit, Niccolo Cabeo, S.J. **Fabri,** by the way, spoke of another of Galileo's problems, the motion of the earth around the sun. His observations, however, came at an awkward time. Apparently more was expected of **Fabri** since he belonged to the Holy Office. The TRS quotes him and then comments on his courageous statements concerning the movement of the earth.

> It hath been more than once asked whether they had a demonstration for asserting the motion of the Earth? They durst never yet affirm they had; wherefore nothing hinders but that the Church may understand those scripture-places, that speak of this matter in a literal sense, and declare they should be so understood as long as the contrary is not evinced by any demonstration; which, if perhaps it should be found out by you (which I can hardly believe it will) in this case the Church will not at all scruple to declare, that these places are to be understood in a figurative and improper sense."
>
> Whence this Author concludes, that the said Jesuit assuring us that the inquisition hath not absolutely declared, that those Scripture places are to be understood literally, seeing that the Church may make a contrary declaration, no man ought to scruple to follow the Hypothesis of the Earth's motion, but only forbear to maintain it in public, till the prohibition be called in.[6]

This statement brought Fabri 50 days in prison under Pope Alexander VII, and he was released only by the intervention of Leopold II. He still put a chapter in his *Dialogi physici* (1665) entitled "de motu terrae" (concerning the earth's motion).

Fabri's ingenious quadrature of the cycloid inspired young Leibniz, and Newton first learned of **Grimaldi's** teaching of divergence from the writings of **Fabri.** He was the leader of a circle of mathematicians which led him into friendship with Gassendi, Mersenne, Cassini, LaHire, Descartes and Huygens. The *Journal des Scavans* speaks of **Fabri's** teaching the circulation of blood before William Harvey. The Jesuit Daniel Bartoli, S.J., was another who did not hesitate to praise the works of Galileo while they were still on the Index. He did much to encourage scientific debates and make science available to the general reader,as well as to encourage impartial consideration of scientific evidence. His books were widely read and frequently translated. In his *Dell'huomo di lettere* (Rome, 1659) he encourages the pursuit of scholarship even in the face of hostility, neglect and poverty. He tried to stimulate appreciation of original ideas and to discourage the worship of authority.[7]

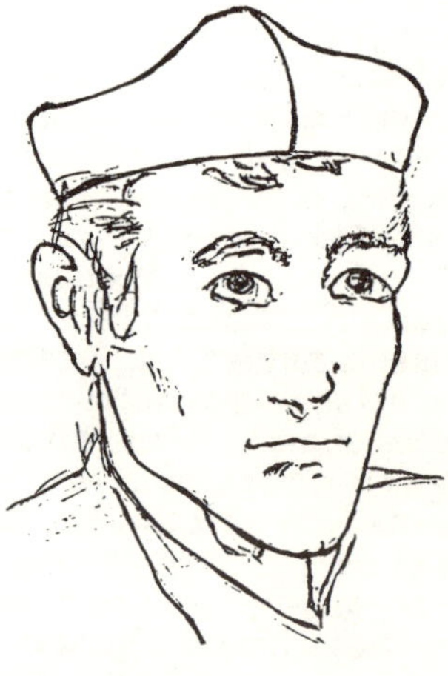

2 Vincent Riccati, S.J. (1707-1775), brother of John, son of Jacob Riccati. "It is fitting that all three are buried in the same vault since their studies were so closely linked during life".

Christopher Scheiner in the training of young mathematicians organized public debates, "disputationes" (many of which were later published), in order to emphasize the geometrical concepts taught. Similarly, **Joseph Stepling** founded a mathematical and scientific research group in Prague which met every month. A large number of treatises of this group were published. In 1753 the Empress Maria Theresa, as part of her educational reform, made him director of the faculty of science and philosophy in Prague.[8]

The Flemish Jesuit **Ferdinand Verbiest** wrote several important geometry books in China, comprising tables, descriptions of instruments and predictions of future eclipses. These writings were treasured by the Emperor.

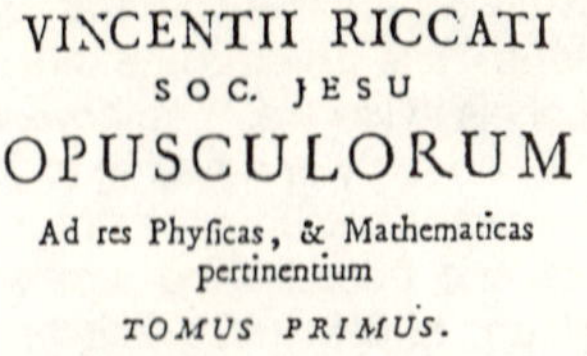
VINCENTII RICCATI
SOC. JESU
OPUSCULORUM
Ad res Phyficas, & Mathematicas pertinentium
TOMUS PRIMUS.

3 Title page of Riccati's *Tomus primus Opusculorum,* which gives the first hint of hyperbolic functions.

c. Their interventions stimulating others to clarify concepts

The heliocentric world system was not widely accepted until 1760, after Copernicus' *De revolutionibus* had been removed from the Index (1757) due to the intervention of **Roger Boscovich**.[9] It was **Boscovich** more than anyone else who finally convinced Pope Benedict XIV to remove Copernicus from the Index of forbidden books, perhaps a century and a half too late.

In the collected works of Robert Boyle and of Christian Huygens and in the correspondence of Isaac Newton, the number of references to Jesuit geometers is extensive. The same can be said of the writings of Descartes, Mersenne, Gassendi and many others. The influence was due in large part to the peculiar position of the Jesuit Society in the field of higher education and to its policy of encouraging scholarship in mathematics among its members. Perhaps because this influence was indirect, it has been ignored by many historians. But frequently Jesuits were able to approach both sides in a dispute and bring a nasty argument to a happy conclusion. Conor Reilly and the DSB illustrate this point.

There were times when some of these men (Jesuits) intervened at critical times. **Pardies** for instance in a growing dispute between Newton and Huygens bringing an unseemly argument to an early conclusion. It was **Roger Boscovich** who finally convinced the Papacy (Benedict XIV) to abrogate the decree of the index against the Copernican system. Some of the elusive language used by Boyle in the early statement of his volume/pressure law was focused because of the intervention of Francis Line.[10]

Pardies intervened at a certain decisive moment in a debate between Newton and Huygens, and his important contributions in his correspondence which reflected a vigorous intellect forced Newton to clarify his thinking. New meanings emerged from beneath the Aristotelian language, and he tried to effect a compromise between Descartes and Aristotle.[11]

4 Ferdinand Verbiest's portrait as one of 108 heroes found in Chinese literature.

The influence of **Clavius** was not limited to his teachings and his enduring books. His correspondence was enormous, and some of it has been collected and preserved in the archives of the Gregorian University in Rome. There are 291 letters - some really treatises - in this **Clavius** collection. Most are from correspondents writing *to* **Clavius**. It is unfortunate that his letters were not saved, but one can still get an idea of his influence. It is, however, like hearing a telephone conversation, able to hear only one party and having to guess at what the other party is asking and saying. The correspondents include not only geometers, but also rulers of all kinds: kings, emperors, and popes. The number and contents of Galileo's letters show that he was a good friend of **Clavius.** The latter was able to joke with him about seeing Jupiter's four moons only because Galileo drew them on the lens of the telescope. Other letters show that **Clavius'** support for Copernicus' heliocentric teaching was the preponderant reason for its acceptance among the learned.

Light is thrown on some personalities in the letters. Tycho Brahe chided **Clavius** for not writing more often. The famous astronomer François Viete was concerned about **Clavius'** criticism because it got him into trouble with Rome. Encyclopedias speak of Viete as a Protestant, a Huguenot, an agnostic, even though he was baptized and died a Catholic. His letters to **Clavius** show him a serious practicing Catholic. Edward Phillips, S.J., has gathered together a commentary on this very interesting collection of letters to **Clavius** illustrating the far reaching influence **Clavius** had.[12]

d. <u>Their efforts to disseminate current geometrical discoveries</u>

The dissemination of geometry throughout the civilized world was evident from the efforts of Father Esprit Pezenas, S.J., a corresponding member of the Academie Royale des Sciences, who played a major role in the diffusion of the geometrical works of the English geometers among the French. The Jesuit Asad Goryu modernized Japanese astronomy and turned it away from the faulty Chinese system. But nowhere is the spread of geometrical ideas more evident than in the works of **Matteo Ricci** and his successors in China, **Schall von Bell** and **Verbiest**. Gilbert Highet comments on the missionary effort and its consequences.

5 Matteo Ricci Johann Schall von Bell Ferdinand Verbiest
The three most prominent leaders of the China mission.

> The Jesuits went to unparalleled lengths and showed unbelievable patience in adapting themselves to the people they had determined to teach. For instance, they sent out a small expedition of ten or twelve priests to Christianize four hundred million Chinese. This almost impossible task they started by studying China. It was an empire, ruled from the top by comparatively few men. Good. If the few men could be converted, the rest would, in due course, follow. Now, how could the few men be converted, the emperor, the courtiers, and the mandarins? What did they admire most? Philosophy, literature , art and science.
>
> The Jesuits therefore spent several years learning Chinese philosophy, art, and literature, making ready to meet the Chinese on their own level. After the imperial officials had slowly, reluctantly admitted them, the Jesuits at once flattered them by talking to them in their own tongue, and attracted them by displaying specially prepared maps and astronomical instruments. Instead of being rejected as foreign barbarians, they were accepted as intelligent and cultivated men. One of them, who became a painter in the Chinese style, is now regarded as one of the classical artists of China.
>
> The next stage, which they approached very, very delicately, was to make the mandarins willing to learn from them. They did this by discussing astronomy with the Chinese scientists, constructing maps of the world with the place-names shown in Chinese characters and the Chinese empire at the center, presenting sundials and astronomical instruments to the high officials whom they met, and ultimately by assisting the Imperial Board of Rites to correct its calendar so as to forecast eclipses and calculate celestial phenomena more accurately than any Chinese had ever been able to do.[13]

From about 1600 until the suppression in 1773, Jesuits were practically the sole source of Chinese knowledge about Western astronomy, geometry and trigonometry

> Appointments in the Astronomical Bureau provided the Jesuits with access to the ruling elite, whose conversion was their main object. Mathematical and astronomical treatises demonstrated high learning and proved that the missionaries were civilized and socially acceptable.[14]

While trigonometry became an analytic science in Europe, in the Orient it remained primitive until the Jesuits came.[15] The China mission has been spoken of with awe and admiration by historians such as Joseph Needham, who relates the difficulties under which the Jesuits labored.

> Ricci, Schall, Verbiest and, in a later generation, Gaubil, were in China at a period of spontaneous decline of indigenous science, the Ming dynasty and early Ching, a decline which had nothing obviously to do with the forces which sent them there and permitted them to stay. . . There was of course the almost insuperable difficulty of language at a time when sinology hardly existed and no good dictionaries had been made.[16]

Another historian of this period was John Baddeley whose book praises the work of the Jesuits even though he disapproves of their motives, - the spread of the Gospel. His frontispiece depicts a Jesuit standing at the left of the throne of the Emperor while all others are kneeling. It has the caption:

> Thrice three times the Envoys bow Forehead to the ground, in vile kowtow:
> The subtle Jesuit flanks the throne, God's, some say - some, the Devil's own.[17]

Matteo Ricci's arrival in China in 1583 marked the beginning of the Catholic missions there. After working in various provinces he finally settled in Peking in 1601, where, under the protection of the emperor Wan-li, he remained until his death. His success was due to his complete adaption to the culture, as well as to his personal qualities and abilities. Recognized as an authority in mathematics and science, he disseminated geometry by lecturing, writing, publishing maps and making scientific instruments. The Chinese geometrical works for which he is remembered were mostly translations of **Clavius'** books on the astrolabe, the sphere, measures and isoperimetrics. But especially important was his Chinese version of the first six books of Euclid's *Elements*, which was written in collaboration with one of his pupils. Entitled *A first textbook of geometry*, this work assures **Ricci** an important place in the history of mathematics.

For 20 years **Ricci** had tried to reach the emperor in person, but the emperor was a recluse not accustomed to seeing his own people. For a time suspicious landlords would drive **Ricci** and his companions from their dwellings, until they hit on the plan of renting haunted houses. Then no one bothered them. Unexpectedly the emperor summoned **Ricci** and his companions to inquire about a ringing clock brought to him by the Jesuits. His own scientists had failed to fix it when it stopped. Since the emperor could not receive these foreigners in person, he had an artist draw full length portraits of them, so that they could have a vicarious interview.

Another opportunity was occasioned by an eclipse of the sun: the prediction of the expected time and duration made by his own Chinese astronomers differed considerably from the Jesuit prediction. When the latter prediction proved correct, the place of the Jesuit mathematicians was secure. It is curious that the Jesuits taught the Chinese the heliocentric theory, unaware that Galileo's trial had taken place. So at the very moment Galileo was being accused of heresy in Rome, the Jesuits in China were teaching the same heliocentric message that they had learned from their Jesuit colleagues before they had left Rome. There was a good five-year lag in communications.

The influence of the China mission was spectacular, including projects like determining the Russo-Chinese border, and its success was even more dramatic than that of the Paraguay Reductions. Their story is told in tapestries and paintings found in the art world and references to them are read in world histories. Europe was thrilled at the venture. Leibniz, an ecumenist far ahead of his time, suggested to his Jesuit friends on the China mission how to clarify the mystery of the Trinity by using the newly discovered imaginary numbers as an analog. It is not clear whether this was ever attempted. Louis XIV was so enthusiastic about the work of this mission that at his own expense he equipped a Jesuit group of "Royal Mathematicians" with the latest scientific instruments and paid their passage to Peking. One of these men, Father Gerbillon, S.J., mapped out the whole Chinese empire; his work is considered a masterpiece even today. His 120 pages of maps have served as the basis of maps of China for the past three centuries.

Although the mission had frightful dangers, savage martyrdoms and terrible disappointments, there were times when the Jesuits enjoyed great prestige, independence and authority. One such time, during the reign of Emperor K'ang Hsi, was the tenure of **Ferdinand Verbiest** (whose Chinese name was *Nan-huai-jen*) as president of the Board of Mathematics. He succeeded **Matteo Ricci** and **Adam Schall** as one of the three great figures of the Jesuit Chinese Mission. Verbiest died 300 years ago on the 27th of January in 1688, was buried with the same imperial honors as the other two, and was laid to rest at their side.

Verbiest had been summoned to Peking by the Mandarin Emperor to succeed **Schall** in his declining years. When he arrived he found himself engaged in a contest with the state astronomer, a Chinese Moslem named Yang-kiang-sien, concerning the position of the planet Mercury. In a public dispute **Verbiest** correctly predicted its location but Yang's prediction proved incorrect. This meant death for the Moslem astronomer, but **Schall** intervened to spare his life.

Charitable though this was, it led to one of the bitterest battles in the history of the mission, in which Yang sought revenge for his humiliation. He registered a triple indictment accusing the mission of being a menace to the state, charging the Jesuits with treason, teaching a false religion and teaching false astronomy. **Verbiest** gave a passionate defense of **Schall**, who by this time was paralyzed and unable to speak. The first charge was not sustained, but the second charge held, so the Jesuits and their Chinese allies were chained and cast into a filthy prison, where they were bound to wooden pegs in such a way that they could neither stand nor sit. There they remained for almost two months until their sentence of strangulation was imposed. A high court found the sentence too light and ordered **Schall** to be cut up into bits while still alive. The sentence, however, was not carried out because an earthquake destroyed the part of the palace chosen for the execution.

Later the government decided to test the third charge of false astronomical teachings. The Emperor ordered a public debate on the relative merits of Chinese and European astronomy. It was to have three parts: to determine the shadow of a fixed gnomon (a column erected perpendicular to the horizon used to find the meridian altitude), to predict the position of the planets at a fixed time and to predict the exact time of a lunar eclipse which was expected about that time. It was decided that the two astronomers, the Chinese Moslem Yang, and the Christian **Verbiest**, should each use his mathematical skills and then the Heavens would be the judge.

The affair was carried out at the Bureau of Astronomy, where were gathered the privy council, the ministers of state, the officials of the observatory, and a host of other mandarins. The inept Yang was not up to the tasks and so **Verbiest**, with his precise data, triumphed in all three. **Verbiest** was immediately installed as president of the Board of Mathematics. The displaced president of the board, having supported Yang, lost face and was banished.

Verbiest then boldly suggested that the mistakes in the calendar be corrected. The Jesuits had reviewed the previous work of the Moslem and Chinese astronomers and proved that an extra month had been inserted. **Verbiest** insisted that it be eliminated. Alarmed that such a public document as the calendar,which had been approved and promulgated by the Emperor, should be altered, the officials begged **Verbiest** to withdraw the suggestion. He replied, "It is not within my power to make the heavens agree with your calendar. The extra month must be taken out." It was, and **Verbiest** had won an astonishing victory.

After this **Verbiest** had a real friend in the Emperor K'ang Hsi, who was eager to share his knowledge. **Verbiest** taught him geometry, and in doing so translated the first six books of Euclid into Manchu. He instructed him also in philosophy and music. In doing this he took advantage of every opportunity to introduce Christianity. The Emperor elevated him to the highest grade of the mandarinate and gave him permission to preach Christianity anywhere in the empire.

After his initial triumphs **Verbiest** was entrusted with very many projects of the empire. It seemed that little went on in the empire during the next few decades without **Verbiest**, and it was not unusual for the Emperor to take **Verbiest** along on his excursions. Having restructured the calendar, one of the empire's most crucial documents, he composed a table of all solar and lunar eclipses for the next 2000 years. Delighted with this the Emperor gave him complete charge of the imperial astronomy observatory, which had been built in 1279.

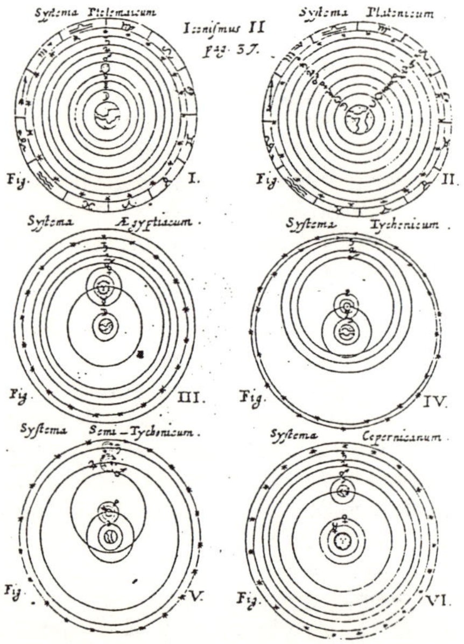

6 From Kircher's *Iter exstaticum coeleste,* a collection of the six prominent theories of planetary motion according to Ptolemy, Plato, Egypt, Tycho, semi-Tycho and Copernicus.

Since the ancient equipment was by now obsolete, **Verbiest** designed new instruments and completely rebuilt the observatory in 1673. Sensitive to the history of the empire, he preserved the old equipment. Then he constructed the great bronze astronomical instruments which have become a Peking tourist attraction even today. When the Jesuits were forced out after the suppression of the Society, the observatory fell into disrepair; during the Boxer rebellion instruments were stolen and brought to Prussia, and the Jesuit scientific library was given to the Czar. In 1981, however, the Chinese government restored the observatory.

His scientific achievements occasioned several princes and many mandarins and scholars to become Catholics, so that by the time **Verbiest** died there were about 800,000 Catholics living in 1,200 communities. His funeral was a very stately affair led by a 25-foot banner telling of his accomplishments. Taking part were fifty horsemen, musicians and standard bearers carrying portraits of **Fr. Verbiest** and the saints. Attending were very many people, including representatives from the Emperor.

Verbiest is listed as one of 108 Chinese heroes in the popular novel *Shui Hu Chuan*, and his portrait is shown with Chinese features in a famous Japanese print. After he died he was buried next to the other two giants of the Jesuit mission, **Matteo**

Ricci and **Adam Schall.** Today it is possible, though difficult, to visit their tomb since it is on the campus of a college of political science, but it is immaculately preserved.

Verbiest died a century after the Jesuit mission had begun, and a century before the tragic decision of Pope Clement XI regarding the Chinese rites, which practically ended this vibrant, promising mission. The work in China had to be started over again in a later century and with much less success. It is not difficult to imagine the consequences if such a decision had been made in the fifth century, when St. Patrick was trying to cope with the rites of the Gaels.

An important vehicle for the dissemination of geometrical ideas was the intellectual apostolate instigated by a Jesuit alumnus, the Minim friar Marin Mersenne. It was a group of intellectuals, including Jesuits, whose intercommunication of ideas was facilitated by Mersenne. His correspondence is contained in a 12-volume work, which stands as a monument to his influence in disseminating geometry throughout Europe.

> From about 1623 Mersenne began to make the careful selection of savants who met at his convent in Paris or corresponded with him from all over Europe and as far afield as Tunisia, Syria, and Constantinople. His regular visitors or correspondents came to include Peiresc, Gassendi, Descartes, . . . Fermat and Pascal. Mersenne's role as secretary of the republic of scientific letters, with a strong point of view of his own, became institutionalized in the Academia Parisiensis, which he organized in 1635 - his monument as an architect of the European scientific community.[18]

Chapter 5 Footnotes

1. Edward Phillips: "The proposals of Father Christopher Clavius for improving the teaching of mathematics" in the *Bulletin of the American Association of Jesuit Scientists.* 1941, vol. 18, p. 203-207.
   Phillips takes this material from the Monumenta Paedagogica S.J., p 471-476 #35,35.
2. TRS vol. 9, p. 229.
3. TRS vol. 3, p. 869.
4. TRS vol. 3, p. 876.
5. TRS vol. 1, p. 325.
6. TRS vol. 1, p. 74-75.
7. DSB vol. 1, p. 483-484. Daniel Bartoli admonished his readers to prove things for themselves and not just to rely on an argument from authority. He wrote several books on physics, on the propagation of sound and on atmospheric pressure.
8. DSB vol. 12, p. 39.
9. DSB vol. 14, p. 159.
10. Conor Reilly: *Francis Line, S.J., an exiled English scientist.* Rome: IHSI,1969, p. 109-110.
11. DSB vol 10, p. 315.
12. Edward Phillips: "The Correspondence of Father Christopher Clavius, S.J., preserved in the Archives of the Gregorian University" in *AHSI* vol. 8, 1939, p. 193-222.
    The influence Clavius - and other Jesuits - had on the direction science and

mathematics took during this time is more fully treated by Peter Dear in "Jesuit mathematical science and the reconstitution of experience in the early seventeenth century" in *Studies in History and Philosophy of Science*, 1987, vol. 18, p.133-175.

13. Gilbert Highet: *The Art of Teaching*. New York: Knopf, 1954, p. 222-223.
14. DSB vol. 14, p. 159.
15. D. E. Smith: *History of Mathematics*. New York: Dover,1958, p. 613.
16. Joseph Needham: *Civilization in China*. vol. 3 Cambridge: University Press, 1959, p. 173.
17. John F. Baddeley: *Russia, Mongolia, China, 1602-1676.* New York: Burt Franklin, 1916. Throughout this classic work on Sino-Russian relations are found references to the work of the Jesuit geometers, including a very respectful biography of Verbiest written by Baddeley himself, "since none is available." (p. 433-437).
18. DSB vol. 9, p. 316.

Chapter 6 Evaluation by Other Geometers

The esteem in which Jesuit geometers have been held over the centuries is evident from what has been written about them in their own time as well as today. The evidence is presented under the following six headings.

a. In learned journals of that period
b. In the histories of that period
c. By their membership in learned societies of that period
d. By their engaging in controversies with other geometers
e. In recent histories, books and commemorations

a. In learned journals of that period

How highly respected they were in their own day is evident from the frequency with which Jesuit geometers' own works as well as commentaries on their works appear in learned journals such as the *Philosophical Transactions of the Royal Society* (TRS) and the *Journal des Scavans.* Their names appear frequently in the early histories of mathematics and are listed in the learned societies such as Academie Royale des Sciences. How seriously their opinions were taken is seen in their many public controversies with other geometers. Today's appreciation is seen in the encyclopedias and in the numerous books written about them, in particular the Dictionary of Scientific Biography (DSB).

The TRS performed a very important function, that of scientific reporting. It made widely available information formerly communicated to only a few individuals by private correspondence. The *Transactions* were an immediate success, both at home and aboard. The first editor, Henry Oldenburg, had created a new field of literature, which was rapidly extended because the *Transactions* was the first journal to print original communications.

Conor Reilly[1] has collected the references to Jesuit works in the TRS for the early 17th Century, and these include some rather remarkable items. For instance, an apology to the readers was needed for any intercommunication with Jesuits.

> Whose goal . . . is to propagate their faith, and to greaten and enrich themselves by their craft; though I deny not but some of them are also ingenious and curious in the matters of a philosophical nature; these that are so, are, I doubt not, obliged to communicate them to heretics, except they were sure they would be well requited for it.[2]

To emphasize this point John Beale once wrote a letter flattering Robert Boyle for his positive influence on these impossible, obdurate men, the Jesuits.

> I am confident that by your philosophy you have converted these very Jesuits to make some recompense for the destruction they have so long made of mankind, that by their universal commerce, incessant industry, and bottomless purses we may receive useful intelligence and experimental formation from all parts of the world.[3]

Some Jesuit publications were translated and presented to the Royal Society by famous people such as Robert Hooke, Robert Boyle and Samuel Johnson. Thomas Birch's *History of the Royal Society*[4] gives interesting connections between Jesuits and the Royal Society and it is to the credit of the first secretary, Henry Oldenburg, that, despite his undeniable personal prejudices, he did not refrain from including accounts of the "undertakings and labors" of considerable numbers of Jesuits. Actually it would have required a special effort to neglect them, because at that time Jesuits were astonishing Europe with their geographical and intellectual discoveries. New lands were still being discovered, people were eager for information about them, and Jesuits were in the forefront of both the exploration and the articulate reporting of their findings. It was obvious that their world-wide organization of highly educated men would be in a very favorable position for sending back valuable information to Europe. Oldenburg was well aware of the possibilities and made many efforts to enlist Jesuits among his overseas correspondents. So he was pleased when **Ignace Pardies** wrote, showing interest in the TRS. He replied, expressing his satisfaction at the prospect of having the French Jesuit as a continental correspondent.

> Especially as those of your celebrated Society (the Jesuits) have the advantage of making, by means of your international correspondence, numerous excellent and useful observations on Nature and the Arts.[5]

In 1701, when the first reorganization of the *Journal des Savants* was taking place, the Jesuits were completing arrangements to publish their own Jesuit periodical *Memoires pour l'histoire des sciences et des beaux-arts*, or, as it came to be known to contemporaries, the *Journal de Trévoux.* The Jesuits who planned the new periodical were members of the faculty of the College of Louis-le-Grand in Paris, the most famous of the Jesuit schools in France. It was later to be the school attended by "the father of modern mathematics," Evariste Galois.

Like the *Journal des Savants,* after which it had been modeled, the Jesuit *Journal de Trévoux* was a literary journal published chiefly for the lettered class in France. The new journal would be dedicated to the advancement of interest in the arts and the sciences; its aim would be to satisfy the intellectual interests of the learned. The largest part of each monthly issue was to consist of summaries and excerpts of all the important books recently published, but if significant original articles were made available to the editors, these too would be published.

1600	1633	1667	1700
Adrianus Romanus, Ld. Bacon, Barlaam, Bayer, Beaugrand, de Beaune, Briggs, Van Ceulen, Descartes, De Dominis, Galileo, Gassendi, Gellibrand, Guldin, Harriot, Horrox, Kepler, Longomontanus, Valerius Lucas, Mydorgius, Metius, Napier, Otho, Oughtred, Leond. da Vinci, Pitiscus, Planudes, B. Porta, Scheiner, Stevin, Torricelli, B. Ursinus, Wright	Borelli, Bartholin, Ld. Brounker, Bullialdus, Cavallerius, Deschales, Fermat, Frenicle, Albert Girard, Js. and D. Gregory, Henrion, Van Heuraet, Hevelius, Horrebow, Kircher, Mersennus, Niel, Norwood, Pascal, Ricciolus, Roberval, Slusius, Snellius, Tacquet, Tchirnhausen, Gregory St. Vincent, Viviani Vlacq, Wallis, Seth Ward, John de Witt	Amontons, Auzout, Bachet, Barrow, Jas. Bernoulli, Collins, Fagnano, Flamsteed, Guido Grandi, P. Grimaldi, l'Hospital, Van Hudden, Hook, Huygens, Kersey, Kircher, Kinkhuysen, Leibnitz, Lieutaud, Mercator, Molyneux, Mouton, Pell, Picard, Ricci, Roemer, Rolle, Renaldinus, Schooten, Wren	John Bernoulli, de Billy, Bradley, Braikenridge, Dom. and Jas. Cassini, Cotes, Craig, s Gravesande, Halley, la Hire, don George Juan, Keill, Lagny, Laloubere, Lansberg, Maclaurin, Meibomius, Manfredi, Marchetti, Newton, Hugo d'Omerique, Ozanam, Prestet, Reyneau, Saunderson, Saurin, Sterling, Brook Taylor, don Ulloa, Varignon, P. Verbiest, Wolfius

1 Part of historian Bossut's collection of the greatest mathematicians of all time. Jesuit names are underlined. Of his 303 names 16 were Jesuit geometers,in spite of the fact that the Jesuits existed for only 2 of the 27 centuries considered.

b. In the histories of that period

The Jesuit mathematicians were known for their independence and bold innovations, a fact not lost on Bossut, the famous mathematical historian, who lists 303 names in his table of the most eminent mathematicians of all time - from 900 B.C. to 1800 A.D. As has already been mentioned, sixteen on the list of 303 are Jesuits. What is remarkable about this is the fact that the Jesuits existed for only 2 of those 27 centuries. A similar collection of names is found in the works of Montucla, who wrote the first comprehensive history of mathematics.[6] M. Maximilian Marie's *Histoire* lists 6 of the top 59 mathematicians for a period at the beginning of the 17th century. Lalande's famous *Astronomy* (1792) lists many Jesuit geometers and astronomers, as does historian Michael Chasle (d 1880).[7] At the time of the suppression of the Jesuits, 30 of the 130 astronomy observatories in the world were Jesuit observatories.[8] Many of these were taken over by the state and still survive to this day, such as those observatories at Vienna, Heidelberg (then Mannheim), Prague, Vilna, Milan, and Rome.

c. By their membership in learned societies of that period

The Transactions show how seriously the Jesuit geometers were taken, not only because their works were reviewed and commented on, but the Royal Society undertook experiments to decide in the cases of contrary findings. Christiaan Huygens criticized Boyle's explanation of an experiment proposed by **Frances Line** in *De corporum inseparabilitate*. The Royal Society carried out the experiment and ruled in favor of Boyle. A good deal of space was used to describe a dispute between **Honoré Fabri** and John B. Borelli on whether a stone thrown horizontally will hit the ground in a shorter time than if it simply dropped.

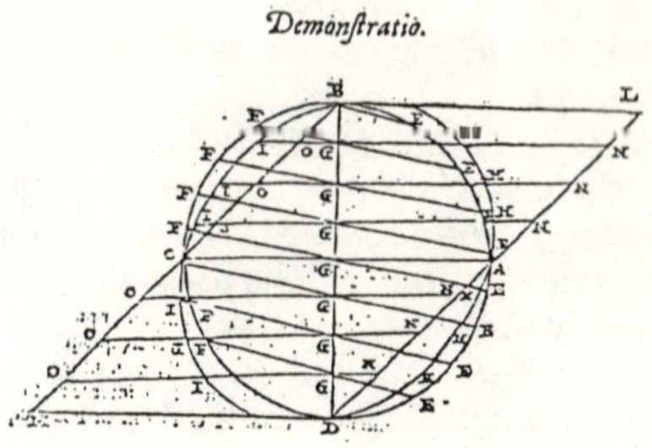

2 Page from the ten-volume work of Gregory St. Vincent, illustrating a step in the disastrous "quadrature of the circle" which proved to be his nemesis.

Hooke's fascination with the "aerial globe" of **Francesco Lana-Terzi** resulted in the construction of a model of the flying ship by the Royal Society. The assertions of **Francis Line** opposing Isaac Newton about light and color led to an investigation favoring Newton. In his *New experiments* Boyle shows familiarity with the works of the Jesuits Acosta, **Kircher, Riccioli, Clavius and Zucchi** and considered them worthy of mention along with Descartes, Pascal, Huygens, Kepler and Galileo.

In Mazovia, a group of Polish Jesuits formed four observatories: in Wilno, in Warsaw, in Poznan, and in Lwow. In France, Jesuit geometers belonged to numerous mathematical organizations, and Joseph Lalande, the great French astronomer said of the Jesuits:

> Among the most absurd calumnies which the rage of the Protestants and Jansenists

> exhale against the Jesuits, I found La Chalotais, who carried his ignorance and blindness to such a point as to say that the Jesuits had never produced any mathematicians. I happened to be just then writing my book on Astronomy and I had concluded my article on 'Jesuit Astronomers' whose number astonishes me. I took the occasion to see La Chalotais on July 20, 1773 and reproached him with his injustice, and he admitted it.[9]

This happened the same year that the Jesuit Society was suppressed.

d. By their engaging in controversies with other geometers

Francis Line entered the Society the year that Robert Southwell was hanged, drawn and quartered. It was a time when those who harbored Jesuits in England were pressed to death. How seriously **Line's** opinions were taken is clear from the reactions of Isaac Newton and Robert Boyle when he attacked their positions, neither of whom were partial to Catholics, especially Jesuits. Boyle had already written a tract *Reasons why a Protestant should not turn Papist: or, Protestant prejudices against the Roman Catholic Religion.*[10]

The academic confrontations between these Jesuit and non-Jesuit scholars had the happy effect of forcing Newton and Boyle to clarify imprecise language. When **Line** persisted in his objections, Newton considered taking up law as a less litigious enterprise.

In 1660 Robert Boyle published his book *New physico-mechanical experiments touching the spring of air*[11] after experimenting with Hooke's vacuum pump. Not only does he give credit to Hooke for building this pump, but he also expresses gratitude to "the industrious Jesuit" **Gaspar Schott** in whose book *Mechanica hydraulica-pneumatica,* he had read the description of the original airpump built by von Guericke. Boyle's book proposes the existence of a vacuum and it was this that brought him into conflict with **Francis Line.**

3 Francesco Maria Grimaldi, S.J., (1613-1663) discovered the diffraction of light, which stimulated Issac Newton's interest, leading to later discoveries.

After Torricelli's experiment with the inverted tube of mercury, the question of a vacuum seemed to be settled in the mind of Robert Boyle. **Francis Line**, however, still clung to the Aristotelian premise that nature abhors a vacuum and so he took issue with Boyle's explanation of the experiment. This led to a prolonged debate between the two, and in the following year, 1661, **Line** published his book *De corporum inseparabilitate* against Robert Boyle's doctrine on the properties of air. Line allowed that air has both spring and weight, but suggested that these two properties were insufficient to account for the phenomena Boyle had described in his *New experiments*. He suggested that air has a third property, the "funiculus" or extremely thin substance, which would not require postulating a vacuum.

This precipitated Boyle's remark in the TRS:

> For this is to be decided not by discourse, but new trial of the Experiment. What it is that imposes upon Mr. Line I cannot imagine: but I suspect he has not tried the Experiment since he acquainted himself with my theory, but depends upon his old notions taken up before he had any hint given to observe the figure of the colored Image. I shall desire him therefore, before he returns any answer, to try it once more for his satisfaction, and that according to this manner.[12]

Then Boyle published his work using the sweeping title: *Defense of the doctrine touching the spring and weight of air . . . against the objections of Franciscus Linus, wherewith the objector's funicular hypothesis is also examined.* Boyle's "spring of air" theory is no more acceptable today than is Line's "funiculus"; it was attractive then only because it was the less absurd of the two explanations. Boyle apologized for the controversy but was convinced to publish by his friends; also since this doctrine was held by the Jesuits, Boyle felt he had to answer it.

> I was more willing to pay them that respect, as not to dissent from persons, divers of whom for their eminence in mathematicks and other learnings I much esteem, without showing that I do it not but upon considerations that I think weighty.[13]

His latter book had the effect of converting **Line** and forcing himself, Boyle, to sharpen his language. In the course of the debate, Boyle showed his esteem, not only for **Line** but for his colleagues "who with much civility wrote against them, never being the least bit antagonistic." He quoted St. Augustine's words against an adversary.

> In mala causa non possunt aliter, at malam causam quis eos coegit habere?[14]
> (You can't change a hopeless case, but who asked you to defend this hopeless case in the first place?)

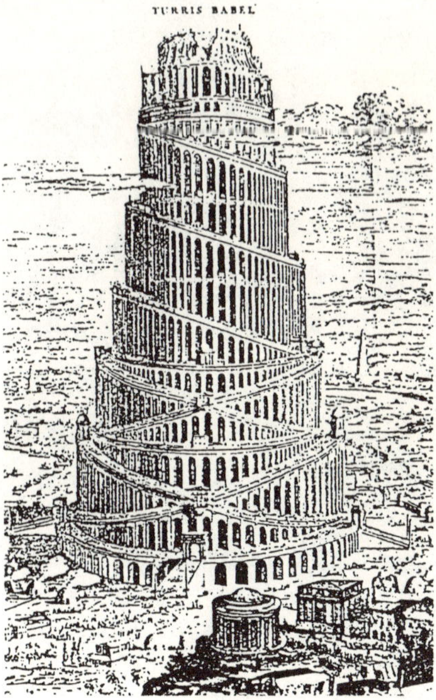

4 Kircher's Tower of Babel: a very familiar picture since copies of this drawing are often found in history books.

In spite of the anti-Jesuit prejudices of his friends (and his own initially), Boyle had a sincere esteem for Jesuits. After vanquishing **Francis Line** he appreciated the fact that **Line** forced him to state (more clearly) what has become ***Boyle's law.*** Boyle's biographer writes, "I do not remember that he had the least antagonism toward **Francis Line** (who with much civility wrote against him)."[15]

Later an elderly **Francis Line** was to get embroiled in a dispute with Isaac

	NASM name	latitude	longitude	diameter
1.	Bettinus	63.4s	315.2e	71.4 km
2.	Billy	13.8s	309.9e	45.7 km
3.	Blancanus	63.6s	338.5e	105.3 km
4.	Boscovich	9.8n	11.1e	46.0 km
5.	Cabaeus	84.9s	324.5e	98.4 km
6.	Clavius	58.4s	345.6e	225.0 km
7.	Cysatus	66.2s	353.9e	48.8 km
8.	De Vico	19.7s	299.8e	20.3 km
9.	Fényi	44.9s	254.9e	39.0 km
10.	Furnerius	36.3s	60.4e	125.2 km
11.	Grimaldi	5.2s	291.4e	410.0 km
12.	Gruemberger	66.9s	350.0e	93.6 km
13.	Hagen	48.3s	135.1e	55.5 km
14.	Hell	32.4s	352.2e	33.3 km
15.	Kircher	67.1s	314.7e	72.5 km
16.	Kugler	53.8s	103.7e	65.8 km
17.	Malapert	84.9s	12.9e	69.0 km
18.	Mayer	63.2n	17.3e	38.0 km
19.	McNally	22.6n	232.8e	47.5 km
20.	Moretus	70.6s	354.5e	114.4 km
21.	Petavius	25.3s	60.4e	176.6 km
22.	Riccioli	3.0s	285.7e	145.5 km
23.	Riccius	36.9s	26.5e	70.6 km
24.	Rodés*	23.0n	283.0e	
25.	Romaña*	21.0s	33.0e	33.6 km
26.	Scheiner	60.5s	332.2e	110.4 km
27.	Schömberger	76.7s	24.9e	85.0 km
28.	Secchi	2.4n	43.5e	22.7 km
29.	Simpelius	73.0s	15.2e	70.4 km
30.	Sirsalis	12.5s	299.6e	42.0 km
31.	Tacquet	16.6n	19.2e	6.6 km
32.	Tannerus	56.4s	22.0e	28.6 km
33.	Zucchius	61.4s	309.7e	64.2 km
34.	Zupus	17.2s	307.7e	38.0 km
35.	Stein	7.2n	179.0e	33.7 km

* Not found in (NASM) catalog but is in the1960 Wilkins Moon Map

	name in Sommervogel	nationality	born time/city	died time/city	field
1.	**Mario Bettini**	(Italian)	b 1582 in Bologna	d 1657 in Bologna	math/astr
2.	**Jacques de Billy**	(French)	b 1602 in Compiegne	d 1679 in Dijon	math/phys
3.	**Giuseppe Blancani**	(Italian)	b 1566 in Bologne	d 1624 in Parme	math/astr
4.	**Roger J Boscovich**	(Croatian)	b 1711 in Ragusa	d 1787 in Milan	math/phys
5.	**Nicolas Cabel**	(Italian)	b 1586 in Ferrare	d 1650 in Genes	phys/astr
6.	**Christophe Clavius**	(German)	b 1538 in Bamberg	d 1612 in Rome	math/phys
7.	**Jean-Baptiste Cysat**	(Swiss)	b 1588 in Lucerne	d 1657 in Lucerne	math/phys
8.	**François de Vico**	(French)	b 1805 in Macerata	d 1848 in London	astr
9.	**Gyula Fényi**	(Hungarian)	b 1845	d 1927	astr
10.	**George Fournier**	(French)	b 1595 in Caen	d 1652 in la Fleche	math
11.	**Francesco Grimaldi**	(Italian)	b 1613 in Bologna	d 1663 in Bolognia	phys
12.	**Chris. Grienberger**	(Swiss)	b1564 in Tyrol	d 1636 in Rome	astr
13.	**Johann Hagen**	(Austrian)	b 1847 in Bregenz	d 1930 in Rome	astr
14.	**Maximilian Hell**	(Hungarian)	b 1720 in Schemnitz	d 1792 in Vienna	phys/astr
15.	**Athanasius Kircher**	(German)	b 1602 in Geisa	d 1680 in Rome	science
16.	**Francis X Kugler**	(German)	b 1862 in Konigsburg	d 1929 in Lucern	hist/math
17.	**Charles Malapert**	(French)	b 1580 in Mons	d 1630 in Victoria	math/philos
18.	**Christian Mayer**	(German)	b 1719	d 1783	astr/math
19.	**Paul McNally**	(American)	b 1890	d 1955	astr
20.	**Theodore Moretus**	(Belgian)	b 1601 in Antwerp	d 1667 in Breslau	math
21.	**Denis Petau**	(French)	b 1583 in Orleans	d 1652 in Paris	hist/astr
22.	**Jean-Bap. Riccioli**	(Italian)	b 1598 in Ferrara	d 1671in Bologna	selenograph
23.	**Matteo Ricci**	(Italian)	b 1552 in Mavrata	d 1610 in Peking	math/geog
24.	**Rodés***	(Hungarian)	b 1881	d 1939	astr
25.	**Romaña***	(Spanish)			astr
26.	**Christophe Scheiner**	(German)	b 1575 in Wald	d 1650 in Neiss	math/phys
27.	**George Schömberger**	(German)	b 1597 in Innsbruck	d 1645 in Hradisch	math/astr
28.	**Ange Secchi**	(Italian)	b 1818 in Reggio	d 1878 in Rome	astrophys
29.	**Hughues Semple**	(Scottish)	b 1596 in Ecosse	d 1654 in Madrid	math
30.	**Gerolamo Sirsalis**	(Italian)	b 1584	d 1654	selenography
31.	**André Tacquet**	(Belgian)	b 1612 in Antwerp	d 1660 in Antwerp	math
32.	**Adam Tannerus**	(Austrian)	b 1572 in Innsbruck	d 1632 in Tyrol	math/theol
33.	**Nicolas Zucchi**	(Italian)	b 1586 in Parmo	d 1670 in Rome	math/astr
34.	**Jean-Baptiste Zupi**	(Italian)	b 1590 in Catanzaro	d 1650 in Naples	astr
35.	**Johan Stein**	(Dutch)	b 1871 in Grave	d 1951 in Rome	astr/phy

Other Jesuits who had craters named for them previously but now are not found on any maps today:

36.	**Andre Arzet**	(French)	b 1604 in Constance	d 1675 in Constance
37.	**Daniello Bartoli**	(Italian)	b 1608 in Ferrara	d 1685 in Rome
38.	**Jean Derienes**	(French)	b 1591 in Dieppe	d 1662 la Fleche
39.	**Rivas**			
40.	**Tibor**			

6 Two lists of the craters named to honor Jesuits: one is taken from the National Air and Space Museum (NASM) catalog, the other with vital statistics is from Carl Sommervogel, S.J. Recently the International Astronomical Union (IAU) codified lunar nomenclature eliminating conflicts: 5 Jesuit names were deleted, bringing the present number to 35. There may have been other Jesuit names in the past and there will certainly be more Jesuit names in the future. Numbers are found on the map.

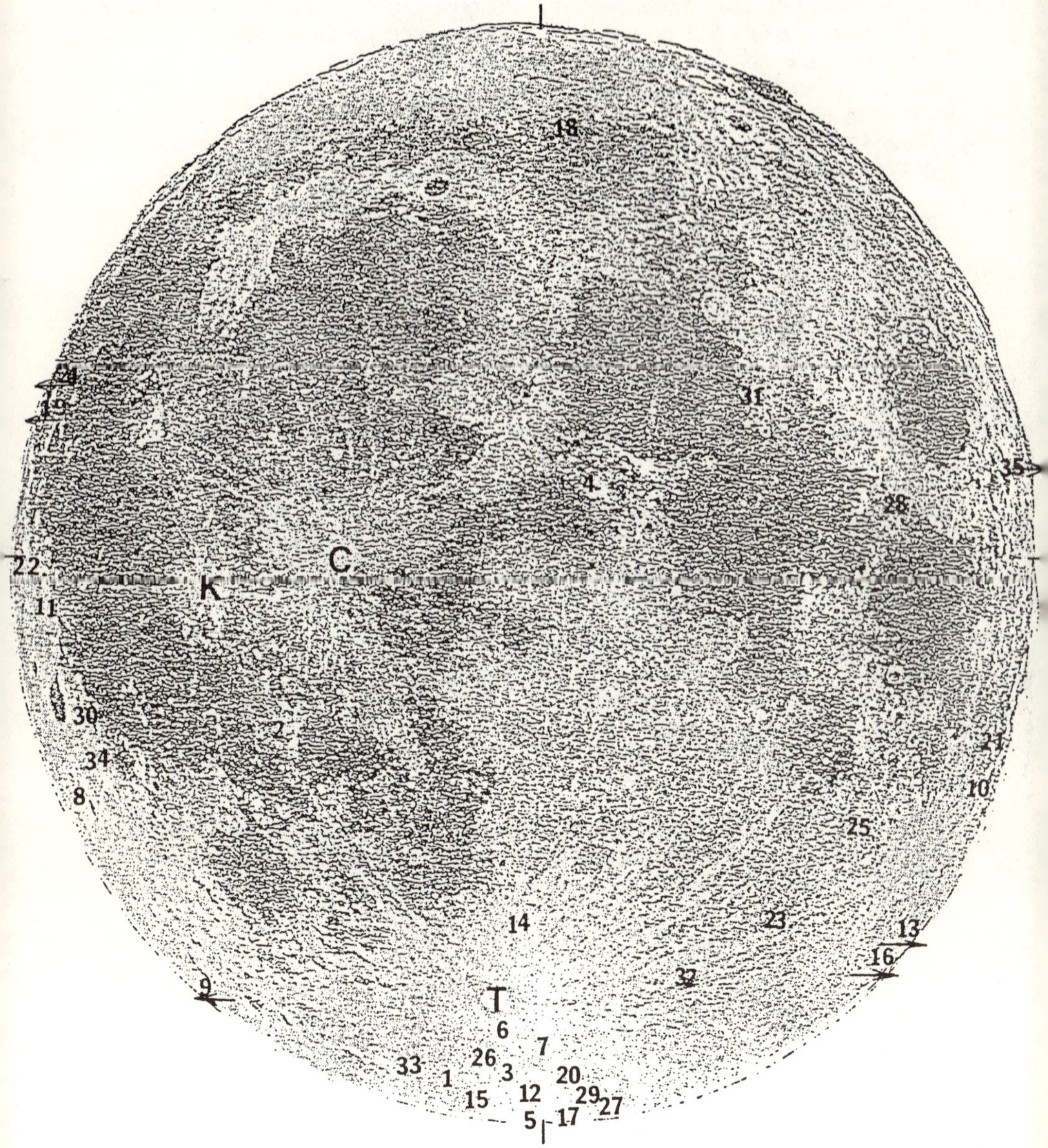

6 Numbered locations of the 35 lunar craters named to honor Jesuits. Some (indicated by arrows) are not visible from earth but are on the far side of the moon. The rest can be located by using as a reference the triangle **KCT** which identifies the three large craters; Kepler, Copernicus and Tycho all of which have distinctive "crater streaks" radiating from them somewhat like the stem of an orange.

Newton over the well-known experiment in geometrical optics in which white light is dispersed into colors after passing through a prism. Newton's explanation centered on the fact that the colors resulted from differing "refrangibility," since the "light of the sun consists of rays differently refrangible." The TRS printed critiques of Newton's theory by Robert Hooke and by the Jesuit **Ignatius Pardies** . . . *some animadversions upon Mr Isaac Newton . . . his Theory of Light* [16] but Newton did not take it well. It is referred to in the TRS as the Newton-Hooke-**Pardies** debate, but it really started with the teachings of **Francesco Maria Grimaldi.** [17] In the course of the correspondence between **Pardies** and Newton published in the TRS, **Pardies** takes his arguments from **Grimaldi,** as does Hooke (who is also one of Newton's sources).[18] **Pardies** had argued that such a drastic departure from the accepted theory should not be entirely founded on the one experiment of the prism since the radical implication of Newton's paper would overthrow the accepted foundations of geometrical optics. But **Pardies** gradually comes to Newton's position, making a rather generous admission of error, which precipitated this reply from Newton:

5 Nicolas Zucchi, S.J. (1586-1670) invented the reflecting telescope and brought one to Kepler in exile.
6 Since 1651 34 Lunar craters have been named after Jesuits. Today only 28 survive: the locations of 26 are seen highlighted here in these two sectors of the moon using the NASA selenograph. Six other Jesuit names have been dropped during revisions of lunar nomenclature since 1922.

> In the observations of Reverend Fr. Pardies, one can hardly determine whether there is more of humility and candor in allowing my arguments their due weight, or penetration and genius in stating objections.[19]

Pardies then clarified some points that had not been clear in his initial treatment. Within a year of his reply to Newton, on April 22, 1673, **Pardies,** at the age of 37, died of a fever caught while ministering to prisoners at Bicetre, near Paris. His death did not go unnoticed among his correspondents in England. At the end of a review of *La Statique* which appeared in the TRS for May 1673, Oldenburg wrote that the book was only part of a work that **Pardies** had planned.

> But since the publications of this part of it we understand that he hath been prevented and cut off by an untimely death; being regretted by those that knew his frankness and strong inclinations to promote philosophical knowledge. How far indeed he hath advanced these other parts of his design, and whether those of his Society, in case he hath made good progress therein, will take care to see it published, we know not but yet hope he hath gone a good way therein, and, if so,

> that his companions will not suppress his labors for the benefit of the young students in this kind of knowledge.[19]

Francis Line pursued **Pardies'** line of objections after **Pardies** met his untimely death. This caused a long dispute with Newton and lasted even until after **Line** died because his pupils continued the correspondence with the TRS and Newton. One of the **Line** letters includes the following defense of **Pardies:**

> Wherefore Mr. Newton had no reason to tax on page 4091 P. Pardies of Hallucination, for making on page 4088, those two Refractions very unequal: For, that learned Optike very well saw, that in a clear day so great an inequality of length and breadth could not be made, unless those two Refractions were also made very unequal. These places, I say, might be added to the former, and further here explicated if need were; but there being no need, I cease to detain you any longer herein.[20]

e. <u>In recent books and commemorations</u>

Historians of mathematics are acquainted with the works of Henri Bosmans, S.J. (1852-1928), who has written about ninety papers concerning mathematicians of the 16th and 17th centuries. Belgian Jesuit mathematicians constituted his special, although not exclusive, interest. His papers are not readily available in the United States, but historian Adolphe Rome, S.J., issued a critical bibliography in ISIS.[21] Many of the Jesuit geometers mentioned here have been reported on and documented by Bosmans in his monographs and to the persistent offer opportunity for further study.

In Dubrovnik is found not only a street named **Boscovich**, but his old school was named after him, and his statue stands on the grounds of Zagreb Atomic Institute. A museum on the island of Lokrum and streets in Milan and Rome are named after **Boscovich.** On the bicentenary of his birth a bust of him was unveiled in Zagreb.

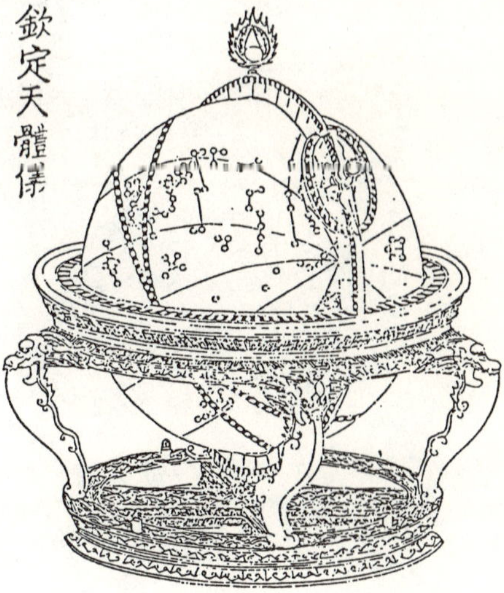

7 The celestial globe constructed by Ferdinand Verbiest for the Royal Observatory of Peking.

Anniversaries have been frequent; in Belgrade 100 articles appeared on the 150th anniversary of his death, and on the bicentenary of his book, *Theoria*, celebrations were held in London and Zagreb. On the bicentenary of his death in 1987 five Symposia were held: in Dubrovnik, in Rome, in Paris, in London and in Milan.

Extraordinary praise has been heaped on this extraordinary Jesuit, a man two centuries ahead of his time, "the commanding genius to whom Rome paid the honor of calling him her master, whom all Italy esteems as a precious treasure, and to whose memory Greece would raise a monument even at the expense of destroying a statue of one of her illustrious heroes. Boscovich is the greatest genius Yugoslavia has ever produced."

> Cassirer considered the Theoria "the leading work in natural philosophy of the eighteenth century." I join Nietzsche in holding it to be "the greatest triumph over the senses that has yet been achieved on earth." But perhaps most important of all is the lucid simplicity of Boscovich's ideas.[22]

The Encyclopedia Britannica in 1801 devoted fourteen pages to **Boscovich's** theory; and the influence of his Theoria was profound in the 19th century. "He was the geometer of atomism, the Euclid of Democritus."[23]

The **Boscovich** archives at Berkeley contains over 180 manuscripts and 2000 pieces of correspondence. The number of **Boscovich** congresses and the number of articles written about him in scientific journals shows an enduring **Boscovichian** revival. "There is a crying need for research on this important eighteenth century polymath," said Professor Roger Hahn of Berkeley. If this is not enough, a crater on the moon is named **Boscovich.**

Thrice three times the Envoys bow
Forehead to ground; in vile kowtow:
The subtle Jesuit flanks the throne,
God's, some say—some, the Devil's own.

8 From the Frontispiece of Baddeley's book on China depicting the influence Jesuits had there - for better or worse.

977. KEPLER AN PAUL GULDIN IN WIEN

Linz, 28. März 1624

Graz, Universitätsbibliothek, Cod. 158, Bl. 2–2b. Eigenhändig

S. P. D.

Reverende Vir. In hoc agone computationum laboris continuj et taediosissimj non mediocriter ṣum recreatus lectione tuarum. Ut igitur tuis etiam occupationibus parcam, parcus ero verborum: nec enim ignorare me sinit circumstantia temporis quae nunc tu construas quae dissolvas problemata.

Vale tandem et ignosce promissioni brevis scripturae fallacj. 28 Martij 1624. Lincij.

R. D. T.

Reverendo Viro, D. Paulo Gulden è Soc.
Jesu Sacerdotj etc. Domino observandissimo.
Wien im Jesuiter Collegio

9 Part of one of Kepler's many letters to Paul Guldin, S.J.

In fact, on the Goddard Space Center selenograph no less than 35 craters are found which are named after Jesuits. They are **Bettini, Billy, Blancanus, Boscovich, Cabaeus, Clavius, Cysatus, DeVico, Fényi, Furnerius, Grimaldi, Grienberger, Hagen, Hell, Kircher, Kugler, Malapert, Mayer, McNally, Moretus, Petavius, Ricci, Riccioli, Rodés, Romana, Scheiner, Schoemberger, Secchi, Simpelius, Sirsalis, Stein, Tannerus, Tacquet, Zucchi, Zupus**. Moreover, until recently five other names have been on past moon maps. They are **Arzet, Bartolius, Deriennes, Rivas and Tibor.**

These names conflicted with other later versions of moon maps and so have been deleted. Today names of scientists throughout the world are nominated for lunar surface features and the decision is made by the International Astronomical Union founded in 1922. But up to this time the basic map for lunar nomenclature was the one mentioned in Chapter **2,** drawn by **Grimaldi** and published by **Riccioli**, the first complete selenograph, and it is found at the entrance to the moon exhibit at the Smithsonian.

Commemorative stamps occasionally remind us of the works of Jesuit geometers. One instance is a beautiful 1983 Belize stamp illustrating the flying ship of "the father of aviation" **Francesco Lana-Terzi**, discussed in chapter 3. It is his own sketch of the proposed airship, four evacuated metal balloons supporting a sailboat with oars.

Occasionally there are exhibitions of Jesuitica which surprise even Jesuits. One such was the exhibition of Jesuit-authored rare science/mathematics books borrowed from the history of science collection housed in one of the best science libraries in the world, The Linda Hall Library in Kansas City, Missouri. Held in 1986, it was a four month display ending on the feast of St. Ignatius, 31 July. The exhibit documented the tremendous scope of Jesuit science in the century of the scientific revolution, and displayed 44 works (not all concerning geometry) of the men mentioned in this book. The introduction states the theme of the exhibition.

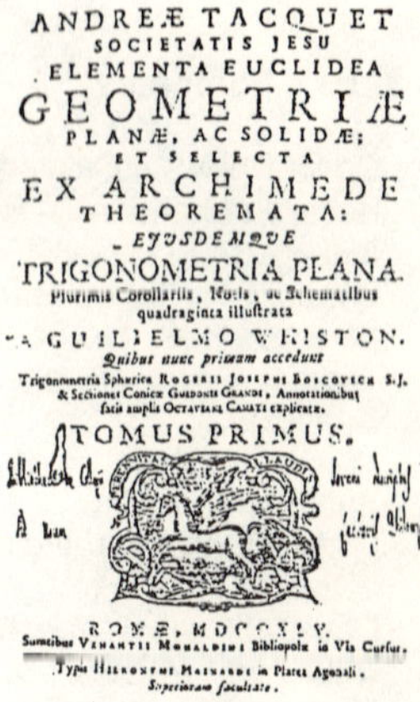
ANDREÆ TACQUET
SOCIETATIS JESU
ELEMENTA EUCLIDEA
GEOMETRIÆ
PLANÆ, AC SOLIDÆ;
ET SELECTA
EX ARCHIMEDE
THEOREMATA:
EJUSDEMQUE
TRIGONOMETRIA PLANA.
Plurimis Corollariis, Notis, ac Schematibus quadraginta illustrata
A GUILIELMO WHISTON.
Quibus nunc primum accedunt
Trigonometria Spherica Rogerii Josephi Boscovich S.J. & Sectiones Conicæ Guidonis Grandi, Annotationibus satis amplis Octaviani Cameti explicatæ.
TOMUS PRIMUS.
ROMÆ, MDCCXLV.
Sumtibus Venantii Monaldini Bibliopolæ in Via Cursus.
Typis Hieronymi Mainardi in Platea Agonali.
Superiorum facultate.

10 Title page for Tacquet's *Elementa geometriae*

> The Society of Jesus in the 17th century contained within its ranks an astonishing number of enthusiastic students of the natural world. Indeed, for the first sixty years of the century, the Jesuits were the only scientific society in existence anywhere. At a time when experimental science was decidedly unfashionable, Jesuits were charting sunspots, calibrating pendulums, timing the fall of weights off towers, and devising a variety of ingenious inventions. Indeed, in the fields of geometry, optics, magnetism, cartography, mechanics, and earth sciences, most of the principal authorities throughout the century were members of the Society of Jesus. The Jesuits were a remarkably bold and imaginative scientific body.[24]

Of course, it must be remembered that these individual endeavors to discover, utilize and promulgate geometry were backed by one organization, the Jesuit Society. It was done before the epoch of "grants in aid" and "foundation funding." Commenting on Jesuit activities, Robert Boyle once remarked:

> Among the Jesuits you know that Clavius and divers others, have as prosperously addicted themselves to mathematics as divinity. And as to physics, not only Scheiner, Aquilonius, Kircher, Schottus, Zucchius and others, have very laudably cultivated the optical and some other parts of philosophy, but Ricciolus himself, the learned compiler of that voluminous and judicious work of the *Almagestum Novum*.[25]

This is as it should be, not only for Jesuit geometers, but also for Jesuit scientists, theologians, philosophers, linguists, historians, and artists according to the tenth and last section of the constitutions of the Society of Jesus. Ignatius Loyola indicated that the Society and its apostolate were to be preserved in the service of others, not only by the spiritual means of zeal and solid virtue but also with diligence and solid learning.[26]

Chapter 6 Footnotes

1. Conor Reilly: "A Catalog of Jesuitica in the Philosophical Transactions of the Royal Society of London" in *Archivum Historicum Societatis Jesu.* 1958, p. 339-362.
2. Ibid., p. 340.
3. Ibid., p. 341 Many readers of the TRS seemed convinced that the Jesuits had vices of heroic degree. Mr. Beale would not be swayed from that tradition.
4. Thomas Birch: *History of the Royal Society.* London: 1756 vol. 2, p. 151.
5. Conor Reilly: *Francis Line, S.J., an exiled English Jesuit.* Rome: I H S I, 1969, p. 109.
6. Maximilian Marie: *Histoire des sciences mathematiques et physiques.* 12 vols. Paris: 1883-1888.
7. Michael Chasle: *Aperçu Historique des methodes en géométrie.* Paris: Gauthier 1875, vol. 2, p. 212.
8. Daniel O'Connell: "Jesuit men of science" in *Studies in Irish literature and science.* Dublin: vol.44, 1955, p. 5.
9. Thomas Campbell: *The Jesuits 1534-1921.* New York: Encyclopedia, 1921, p. 355.
10. Louis More: *Life and works of the honourable Robert Boyle.* London: Oxford, 1944, p. 167. The author, who is rather hostile to Line, defends the claim that Boyle wrote this tract, even though it was presented anonymously.
11. Ibid., p. 243n. Boyle supposes that particles of air were like tiny coiled watch springs, each having a complicated circular motion to explain phenomena like rarefaction and condensation. This was to offset the "funiculus" theory of Line.
12. TRS, vol. 10 p. 500.
13. Conor Reilly: *Francis Line* op.cit., p. 72.
14. Ibid., p. 83.
15. Ibid., p. 79.
16. TRS, April 9,1672.
17. Reilly: op.cit., p. 107.
18 Reilly: op.cit., p. 111.
19. TRS, vol. 7, 1672 p. 5012.
20. TRS, vol. 10, p. 501.
21. ISIS, vol. 12, 1929 p. 100-112.
22. Lancelot Whyte: *Roger Joseph Boscovich,* New York: Fordham, 1961, p. 124.
23. Ibid., p. 105,107.
24. William B. Ashworth: *Jesuit science in the age of Galileo.* Kansas City: Lowell Press p. 5.
25. Thomas Birch: *The works of the honourable Robert Boyle.* 5 vols. London:1744, vol. 4 p. 62.
26. Ignatius Loyola: *The Constitutions of the Society of Jesus.* (Translated by George E. Ganss, S.J.) St Louis: The Institute of Jesuit Sources, 1970, Part X, 3, #814, p. 333.

References and sources

1. *Archivum Historicum Societatis Iesu* (AHSI) Rome: Institutum Historicum
2. Attwater, Rachel *Adam Schall*. Milwaukee: 1963
3. Bangert, William *A History of the Society of Jesus.* St. Louis: St. Louis Institute, 1972
4. Bossut, Charles *Essai sur l'histoire générale des mathématiques.* Paris: 1802
5. Bossut, Charles *Histoire générale des mathématiques.* Paris: F. Louis, 1810
6. Boyer, Carl *History of the calculus.* New York: Columbia, 1939
7. Boyer, Carl *History of analytic geometry.* New York: Scripta Mathematica, 1956
8. Boyer, Carl *A history of mathematics.* New York: Wiley, 1968
9. Burke-Gaffney, M. W. *Kepler and the Jesuits.* Milwaukee: Bruce, 1944,
10. Cajori, Florian *A history of mathematical notations* 2 vols. Chicago: Open Court, 1928
11. Cajori, Florian *A history of mathematics*, New York: Macmillan, 1919
12. Cantor, Moritz *Vorslesungen uber geschichte der mathematik.* 4 vol. Leipzig: Teubner,1892-1908
13. Chasles, Michel *Traité de géométrie superieure.* Paris: 1852
14. Child, J. M. *The early mathematical manuscripts of Leibniz.* Chicago: Open Court, 1920
15. Debus, A. G. ed., *World Who's Who in Science.* Chicago: Marquis,1968
16. Duhr, Bernhard, S.J. *Geschichte der jesuiten in den landern deutscher zunge (in der ersten halfte des XVII Jahrhunderts).* Berlin: 1913
17. *The Encyclopedia Britannica.* 24 vols. Chicago. Benton, 1959
18. Gillispie, Charles. C. ed., *Dictionary of Scientific biography.* 16 vols. New York: Charles Scribner and Sons, 1970
19. Godwin, Josceln *Athanasius Kircher.* London: Thames & Hudson, 1979
20. *Grande Larousse encyclopédie.* 10 vols. Paris: Libraire Larousse, 1960
21. Gallagher, Louis *China in 16th Century: journals of Matthew Ricci* New York: 1953
22. Highet, Gilbert *The art of teaching.* New York: Knopf, 1954
23. Kaestner, Abraham Gotthelf: *Geschichte der mathematik.* 4 vols. Goettinger: Rosenbusch, 1796-1800
24. Kline, Morris *Mathematical thought from ancient to modern times.* New York: Oxford, 1972
25. Koch, Ludwig ed., *Jesuiten-Lexikon.* 2 vols. Waversebaan, Belgium: Lowen-Heverlee,1962
26. Kramer, Edna *The nature and growth of mathematics.* New York: Hawthorne, 1970
27. Larousse, Pierre *Grand Dictionnaire Universel. 17 vols.* Paris: Grand Dictionaire-Universel, 1865
28. Le Grande, Pierre *Journal des Savants (scavans).* Amsterdam: 1665-1714
29. Loria, Gino *Storia delle matematiche,* 3 vols. Turin: 1929-1933
30. Marie, Maximillien *Histoire des sciences mathématiques et physiques.* 12 vols. Paris: 1883-1888
31. Montucla, Etienne *Histoire des mathématiques.* 4 vols. Paris: Henri Agasse, 1798-1799
32. Naux, Charles *Histoire des logarithms de Neper a Euler.* 2 vols. Paris: Libraire Scientifiques, 1971
33. Newman, James *The World of Mathematics.* 4 vols. New York: Simon & Schuster, 1956
34. Oldenburg, Henry ed. *Philosophical Transactions of the Royal Society.* vols. 1-30. London: 1665-1715

35. Reilly, Conor "A catalogue of Jesuitica in the Philosophical Transactions of the Royal Society of London" in A.H.S.I. vol. 27,1958, p. 339-362
36. Reilly, Conor *Francis Line, S.J. an exiled English scientist 1595-1675.* Rome: Institutum Historicum, 1969.
37. Reilly, Conor *Studia Kircheriana.* Wiesbaden: Edizioni del Mondo, 1974
38. Rigaud, S. ed. *Correspondence of scientific men of the seventeenth century.* 2 vol. London: Oxford University Press, 1841
39. Sarton, George *The study of the history of mathematics.* Cambridge, Mass: Harvard, 1936
40. Smith, D. E. *Source book in mathematics.* New York: McGraw-Hill, 1929
41. Smith, D. E. *History of mathematics.* New York: Dover, 1958
42. Sommervogel, Carolus *Bibliothèque de la compagnie de Jésus.* 12 vols. Bruxelles: Société Belge de Libraire, 1890-1960
43. Struik, D. J. *A concise history of mathematics.* 2 vols., New York: Dover, 1948
44. Struik, D. J. ed., *A source book in mathematics, 1200-1800.* New Jersey: Princeton, 1969
45. Trescani, Giovanni *Enciclopedia italiana.* Milan: Rizzoli, 1936
46. Wallace, William *Galileo's early notebooks.* Notre Dame: Notre Dame Press, 1977
47. Whyte, Lancelot *Roger Joseph Boscovich, S.J., F.R.S. 1711-1787.* New York: Fordham, 1961
48. Wittkower, Rudolf & Jaffe, Irma *Baroque art: the Jesuit contribution.* New York: Fordham, 1972
49. Wolf, A. *A History of science, technology and philosophy in the 16th and 17th centuries.* New York: Macmillan, 1959
50. Wolf, A. *A History of science, technology and philosophy in the 18th century.* London: 1938
51. Ziggelaar, August *François de Aguilon, S.J. (1567-1617) scientist and architect.* Rome: Institutum Historicum, 1983

Appendix 1

56 Prominent Jesuit Geometers

Here is a brief description of the lives and some of the geometrical works of the 56 better-known Jesuit geometers, taken from Sommervogel. There is little point in giving a page reference to Sommervogel since all are listed in alphabetical order. Because of the variety of spellings, the Sommervogel versions are used here. References to professional journals such as the *Dictionary of Scientific Biography* (DSB), the *Philosophical Transactions of the Royal Society of London* (TRS) and *Le Journal des Savants* (also "Scavans": JSV) are indicated for further reading. The number of entries in Sommervogel does not always correspond to the number of books the man has written, since Sommervogel does not list all publications and also some of the numbers refer to repeated editions. These numbers, however, do give some indication of how busy the man was.

1. François D'Aguilon (French) b 1546 in Brussels d 1617 in Antwerp
Reference to him in the Dictionary of Scientific Biography is found in v 1 p81, and v12 p74.
1 entry is found in Sommervogel:
Opticorum libri sex (Antwerp, 1613)
He founded a Belgian school for mathematics in Antwerp. In his work the word "stereographic" to describe the projections of Hipparcus appears for the first time. The first edition of his book, which went into several editions, was dedicated to the governor Inigo Borgia (a relative of Francis Borgia, S.J.). Peter Paul Rubens designed the engravings for the illustrations of the book. D'Aguilon planned to write books on catoptrics and dioptrics but died before he finished them.

2. François X Alegre (Mexican) b 1729 in Vera Cruz d 1788 in Bologna
14 entries are found in Sommervogel; an example is the following:
Elementorum geometriae Lib. XIV sectionum conicarum Lib.IV una cum tractatu de gnomonica (Bologna, 1770)
A crater on the moon was named in his honor: it was found in the sixth octant of the early editions of lunar maps, but has since been renamed. A century (1889) after his death all his unpublished works were collected and published.

3. Joseph M Amiot (French) b 1718 in Toulon d 1793 in Peking
28 entries are found in Sommervogel; some examples are the following:
Art Militaire des Chinois (Paris, 1772) *Dictionnaire Tartar (Paris, 1790)*
Positions géographiques Turkestan (Lyon, 1880)
His specialties included geometry and physics, but he also had great talent for music. He had earned the confidence of the Chinese emperor Kien-Long, and after the suppression he continued his work in Peking with the support of the same French government that suppressed the Jesuits.

4. André Arzet (French) b 1604 in Constance d 1675 in Constance
3 entries are found in Sommervogel; an example is the following:
Clavis Mathematica (Constance, 1634)
He taught in Constance for his whole life and was praised by Riccioli in *Almagistum novum*

for his work on eclipses. A lunar crater was named for him.

5. Mario Bettini (Italian) b 1582 in Bologna d 1657 in Bologna
7 entries are found in Sommervogel; an example is the following:
Aerarium Philosophiae Mathematicae (Bologna, 1648)
He taught the geometry of military art, stereometry and conics. A crater on the moon is named in his honor.

6. Jacques de Billy (French) b 1602 in Compiegne d 1679 in Dijon
Reference to him in the Dictionary of Scientific Biography is found in v 2 p131, v 4 p574, v 5 p528, v 13 p253.
Articles by him or concerning his work are found in the Philosophical Transactions of the Royal Society of London in v 1 p 324, v 2 p 568-575 and v 6 p 2185.
Le Journal des Savants (Scavans) (6 sept.1666) published his method for finding a date in the Julian calender.
15 entries are found in Sommervogel; some examples are the following:
Nova Geometriae Clavis Algebra (Paris, 1643) *Opus Astronomicum (Paris, 1661)*
De Proportione Harmonica (Paris, 1658) *Discours de la Comete (Paris, 1665)*
Doctrinae analyticae inventum novum (Toulouse, 1670)
He taught mathematics at Pont a Mousson, Rheims and finally at Dijon, where he became quite friendly with Fermat. Fermat edited one of his books, while he preserved the algebraic discoveries of Fermat in his *Doctrinae analyticae*. There was abundant correspondence between the two men concerned with topics such as indeterminate analysis, diophantane equations, and harmonic ratios. De Billy is frequently mentioned in Cajori's *History of mathematical notations.*

7. Jean Bonfa (French) b 1638 in Nimes d 1724 in Avignon
Articles by him or concerning his work are found in the Philosophical Transactions of the Royal Society of London in v 14 p715-720, 1686, p175.
Le Journal des Scavans (Jan 1679, p24-26) published his "Lettre touchant une nouvelle invention de faire des pendules," in which he describes some of measuring instruments he invented. His "Binocle Géométrique" was published in the Journal de Trevoux (Jan. 1702).
7 entries are found in Sommervogel; an example is the following:
Carte Geographique du Comète Venaissin (Marseille, 1699)
One of his correspondents, Dominic Cassini, along with others admired his astronomical observations as well as his geometrical instruments. He taught mathematics at Avignon and Marseilles.

8. Roger J Boscovich (Croatian) b 1711 in Ragusa d 1787 in Milan
Reference to him in the Dictionary of Scientific Biography is found in v 1 p462, v 2 p326-332, v 3 p156, 539, v 4 p529, v 6 p 86, 335, v 8 p159, 360, v 11 p142, v 12 p608, v 13 p39, 235, 375, v 14 p70, v 15 p309, 352, 376.
108 entries are found in Sommervogel; some examples are the following:
De Circulis Osculatoribus (Rome, 1740) *Trigonometriae sphaericae (Rome, 1737)*
De natura et usu infinitorum (Rome, 1741) *Elementorum Matheseos (Rome, 1752)*
Philosophiae naturalis theoria (Rome, 1758)
Born eighth of nine children, he had an older brother, Barthelemy (1699-1770), who also was a Jesuit mathematician, and on occasion took Roger's place teaching when he was needed elsewhere. He taught at the Roman College for 20 years, although the Jesuit General Luigi Centurione, S.J. (1755-1757) thought his teachings dangerous. When his

admirer Laurence Ricci, S.J., became the Jesuit General, however, Boscovich was made a *Visitor* of the whole Jesuit Society. He did not suffer fools gladly. He argued against some of the Jesuits' blind loyalty to Aristotelean physics; when shown the treasures of the Jesuit school at Sens, which included a rib of the prophet Isaiah, he told the rector to throw it away, in the interest of truth. Correspondent for the Royal Society, he was also a frequent contributor to the Jesuit *Mémoires des Trévoux.* The famous astronomer/mathematician Joseph Lalande said there was no scholar in all Italy like Boscovich nor did he know any geometer as profound. After the suppression Lalande accompanied Boscovich on a journey through France using a *salvus conductus* (safe-conduct pass) given Boscovich by Louis XV.

He developed the first coherent description of atomic theory in his work *Theoria Philosophiae Naturalis*, which is one of the great attempts to explain the universe in a single idea. His influence on modern atomic physics is undoubted, and his works are kept as the Boscovich Archives in the Bancroft Library of Rare Books at Berkeley. On the anniversaries of his publications, his birth, and his death, symposia are held throughout the world to honor this amazing polymath.

Boscovich was a creative scientist whose inventions included the ring micrometer and the achromatic telescope. He was the first to apply probability to the theory of errors, as was later acknowledged by Laplace and Gauss. It was his influence that minimized the hostility of Catholic churchmen to the Copernican system, and he convinced Pope Benedict XIV to remove Copernicus from the Index of Forbidden Books. During his life he had been commissioned by popes and emperors to do such jobs as repair the fissures in St Peter's dome as well as other cathedral domes, direct the drainage of the Pontine marshes and survey the meridian of the Papal states.

He traveled very often as a *Visitor* of the Society of Jesus, but also as a geometer. He gathered data to define the shape of the earth while on an excursion to Brazil. Another scientific expedition to California had to be canceled because of growing hostility to the Jesuits. After the suppression of the Jesuits he became captain of optics in the French navy.

Born in Ragusa (now Dubrovnik, Yugoslavia), Boscovich lived a long, fruitful life. Incisive in thought, adventuresome in spirit, and independent in judgment, he was a man of the eighteenth century in some respects, but far ahead of his time in others.

9. Joachim Bouvet (French) b 1662 in Mans d 1732 in Peking
Articles by him or concerning his work are found in the Philosophical Transactions of the Royal Society of London in v 20 p244.
10 entries are found in Sommervogel; an example is the following:
Elementa geometriae (Peking, 1690)

He was one of the party of six Jesuits, along with de Fontaney, Tachard, Visdelou, Lecompte and Gerbillon, who accompanied de Chaumont to Siam in 1685 as "Mathématiciens Royal." He later proceeded to China. His *Portrait de l'Empereur de la Chine* was translated into German by Leibniz in 1699, and an English translation appeared the same year. He was a frequent correspondent of the king's confessor, the Jesuit Père la Chaise (after whom is named the famous cemetery in the middle of Paris).

10. Louis B Castel (French) b1688 in Montpellier d 1757 in Paris
Reference to him in the Dictionary of Scientific Biography is found in v 3 p114-115, v 5 p54, v 5 p510, v 15 p58, v 15 p270.
Articles by him or concerning his work are found in the Philosophical Transactions of the Royal Society of London.

21 entries are found in Sommervogel; some examples are the following:

Plan d'une Mathématique (Paris, 1727) *Mathématique universelle (Paris, 1778)*

Sommervogel lists his correspondence with other mathematicians, 23 articles in *Mémoires des Trévoux* and 13 in *Mercure de France*. The Bibliotheque Royal in Brussells now holds many of his manuscripts. In 1730, he was elected to the Royal Society of London, and to the Bordeaux Academy in 1746, despite his opposition to the teachings of Newton. He reproached Newton with wanting to reduce man to "using only his eyes," because Newton's experimental proofs were all visual. He was especially remembered throughout Europe for his ocular harpsichord, a scheme for making colors and musical tones correspond.

11. Thomas Ceva (Italian) b 1648 in Milan d 1737 in Milan
Reference to him in the Dictionary of Scientific Biography is found in v 2 p182, v 3 p183-184, v 12 p 55.
Articles by him or concerning his work are found in the Philosophical Transactions of the Royal Society of London.
35 entries are found in Sommervogel; some examples are the following:

De cycloide (Milan, 1690) *Opuscula mathematica(Milan, 1699)*

Ceva carried on an extensive correspondence with the famous mathematician Guido Grandi, a Camaldolese monk. An essay of his appears at the end of one of Grandi's works. He invented a device to divide an angle into an arbitrary number of parts; ten years later the device was claimed by L'Hospital, with no mention of Ceva. He brought Newton's theory of gravitation to Italy.

Thomas Ceva was a poet as well as a geometer and his poem "*Jesus Puer*" *(Milan,1690)* went through many printings, was translated into several languages, and occasioned many commentaries. In fact, he has been called "the greatest Jesuit poet-genius." He came from a famous Italian family. "Ceva's theorem" is named for his brother Giovanni.

12. Claude F. M. de Chales (French) b 1621 in Chambery d 1678 in Turin
Reference to him in the Dictionary of Scientific Biography is found in v1 p81, v 3 p621-622, v 4 p452, v 4 p505,v 13 p320.
Articles by him or concerning his work are found in the Philosophical Transactions of the Royal Society of London in v 9 p229-233.
8 entries are found in Sommervogel; some examples are the following:

Euclidis elementorum libri octo (Lyons, 1660)
Cursus seu Mundus Mathematicus (Lyons,1674)
Principles généraux de la géographie mathématique (Paris, 1672)

He was a distinguished mathematician and was appointed Royal Professor of hydrography at Marseilles by Louis XIV. He wrote, as well, on navigation and the art of fortification.

13. Jean Ciermans (Belgian) b 1602 in Bois le duc d 1648 in Portugal
4 entries are found in Sommervogel; some examples are the following:

Repetito menstrua (Louvain, 1639) *Annus Positionum Mathematicarum (Louvain, 1641)*

Anticipating Pascal by a few years, he invented the first calculator capable of adding and subtracting "with no chance of error." He engaged in a well-publicized philosophical dispute with Descartes. His *Repetito menstrua* included a different science for each month and was based on the Moslem calendar. He wanted to work in the China mission but died at the age of 46 in Portugal while on his journey to China.

14. Christopher Clavius (German) b 1538 in Bamberg d 1612 in Rome
Reference to him in the Dictionary of Scientific Biography is found throughout

but especially in v 3 p311-312.
Articles by him or concerning his work are found in the Philosophical Transactions of the Royal Society of London in v 1 p135, v 1 p353-254, v 1 p289-294, v 12 p1030-1035, v 14 p721-726. 24 entries are found in Sommervogel; some examples are the following:

In Sphaeram Joannis de Sacrobosco (Rome, 1570 *Gnomonices libri Octo (Rome, 1581)*
Euclid elementorum (Rome, 1589) *Epitome Arithmeticae practicae (Rome,1584)*
Novi calendarii (Rome, 1588) *Astrolobium (Rome, 1593)*
Geometrica practica (Rome, 1604) *Opera mathematica (Rome, 1611)*

Born before the start of the Society of Jesus, he was one of its earliest members. His name and his date of birth have been incorrectly given by some historians. One such name was Christopher Schluessel (key), but his name in German was Christopher Claus (from klais = key). He was professor of mathematics at the Roman College for forty-five years; and during this time he won the respect and friendship of numerous astronomers and mathematicians, among whom are numbered Viete, Kepler and Galileo. He was a life-long friend of Galileo, and a 1611 report from Clavius and his Jesuit colleagues confirmed Galileo's discoveries. He was an outstanding astronomer and mathematician. He exerted a wide influence on the schools of Europe as well as China through his Jesuit pupils laboring there. The historian of science George Sarton calls him "the most influential teacher of the Renaissance."

Recently (7/6/79) a front page article in the *New York Times* credits "chronicler" Clavius with furnishing the 16th century astronomical records as evidence for Princeton astronomers' claim that the sun was shrinking. A total eclipse of the sun no longer displays the noticeable ring which had been seen by Clavius.

Clavius anticipated a number of mathematical developments: e.g., the decimal point, parenthesis, use of logarithms and the vernier scale. It was Clavius who replaced the Julian calendar with the Gregorian calendar. Later mathematicians such as Leibniz became interested in mathematics by reading his works. In his *Tractatus triangulorum* Clavius summarized nearly all contemporary knowledge of plane and spherical trigonometry. His *Euclidis elementorum* contains all the known books of Euclid and a vast collection of comments and elucidations. Later editions of this work became the standard text in the 16th- and l7th-century European schools. In this work, Clavius showed concern for the axioms of Euclid and noted the absence of an axiom guaranteeing the existence of a fourth proportional to three given magnitudes. This work led to his being called "the Euclid of the l6th Century."

15. Honoré Fabri (French) b 1607 in Dauphine d 1688 in Rome
Reference to him in the Dictionary of Scientific Biography is found in v 4 p505-506, v 5 p544, v 8 p267.
Articles by him or concerning his work are found in the Philosophical Transactions of the Royal Society of London in v 1 p325-327, v 1 p69-73, v 2 p626, v 4 p925-928, v 5 p2055-2057, v 5 p2057-2059, v 5 p2082-2083, v 9 p78-83, v 16 p314-323.
31 entries are found in Sommervogel; some examples are the following:

Theses de universa mathematica (Lyons, 1646) *Philosophis Universa (Lyons, 1646)*
Opusculum geometricum (Rome, 1659) *De Homine (Lyons, 1666)*

He wrote more than thirty works, many of them on scientific topics, some of which were reviewed in the Philosophical Transactions. In his treatise *De Homine* Fabri claimed to have discovered the circulation of the blood prior to Harvey. Sommervogel implies that the most Fabri can claim is that he discovered it without knowing of Harvey's work, since Harvey published so much earlier than Fabri. He was a member of the *Holy Office,* so when he stated his opinion that the Catholic Church would adopt a figurative meaning to the offending biblical passages if it was shown that the earth does indeed move, he was thrown into prison by Pope Alexander VII for 50 days, and even then he was only released because King Ferdinand intervened.

16. Jean C. de la Faille (Belgian) b 1597 in Antwerp d 1654 in Barcelona
Reference to him in the Dictionary of Scientific Biography is found in v 7 p583, v 7 p557-558, v 8 p26, v 12 p436, v 13 p561.
3 entries are found in Sommervogel; some examples are the following:
Theses Mechanicae (Dolae, 1625) *Theoremata de Centro Gravitatis (Antwerp, 1632)*
He taught at the Imperial College. He is the subject of a well-known painting of Van Dyke which stands in the Brussels *Plantin Museum of fine arts;* it was on loan to the New York Metropolitan Museum in 1984. Since he was the tutor of Don Juan of Austria, he went on the latter's campaigns, and met his death during one such battle.

17. Jean de Fontaney (French) b 1645 in Bretagne d 1710 in la Flèche
Articles by him or concerning his work are found in the Philosophical Transactions of the Royal Society of London in v 13 p145-149, v 14 p715-720, v 20 p371-373.
15 entries are found in Sommervogel; an example is the following:
Observations sur la comète (Paris, 1681)
He was professor of mathematics at Clermont College, Paris. He was a distinguished astronomer and a corresponding member of the Académie des Sciences. Fontaney was superior of the group of "Royal Mathematicians" sent by Louis XIV to Siam in 1685. He went on to China, returning to Europe later. In *Le Journal des Scavans* 21 Nov. 1678, pp. 213-6, he is credited with recording an occultation of Saturn along with Cassini, de la Hire and others. He was a correspondent of the famous Jesuit Père la Chaise.

18. Aegidus F. de Gottignies (Belgian) b in Brussels 1630 d 1689 in Rome
Articles by him or concerning his work are found in the Philosophical Transactions of the Royal Society of London in v 1 p209-210, v 5 p2054-2055.
14 entries are found in Sommervogel; some examples are the following:
Elementa Geometriae Planae (Rome, 1669) *Logistica (Rome, 1675)*
Problema duplatio (Rome, 1681) *Logistica Universalis sive mathesis (Naples, 1687)*
Aegidus (Gilles) de Gottignies was sent to study at Rome, and he was later appointed professor of mathematics at the Roman College. He was an industrious scholar of wide interests, and published many scientific works. His correspondence with Cassini concerning the eclipse of Jupiter was published in Bologna in 1665. He published a study on the anatomy of the eye of a fly which was later translated into French by the famous naturalist Buffon.

19. Christopher Grienberger (Swiss) b1564 in Tyrol d 1636 in Rome
9 entries are found in Sommervogel; some examples are the following:
Euclidis sex primi (Rome, 1655) *Elementa trigonometrica (Rome, 1630)*
Correspondent with Galileo as well as with Cardinal Robert Bellarmine, he was Clavius' replacement as professor of mathematics at the Roman College. As such he had to make a difficult decision regarding the publication of St. Vincent's great work, *Opus geometricum.* Grienberger verified Galileo's discovery of the four moons of Jupiter; then later in 1611 he organized a convocation honoring Galileo. At this gathering of cardinals, princes and scholars, the students of Clavius and Grienberger expounded Galileo's discoveries to the delight of Galileo. He is said to have observed that if Galileo had heeded the advice of the Jesuits and proposed his teachings as hypotheses, he could have written on any subject he

wished, including the rotation of the earth.

20. Francesco M Grimaldi (Italian) b 1613 at Bologna d at Bologna 1663
Reference to him in the Dictionary of Scientific Biography is found in v 3 p100, 528, v 4 p506, v 5 p 542, v 6 p 195, 545, v 9 p485, v 10 p59, v 11 p411, v 14 p461.
Articles by him or concerning his work are found in the Philosophical Transactions of the Royal Society of London in v 6 p3069-3070, v 16 p314-323.
2 entries are found in Sommervogel; an example is the following:

Physico-mathesis de Lumine (Bologna, 1665)

He was professor at Bologna for many years, and was one of the great geometer-physicists of his time. He was an exact and skilled observer, especially in the field of optics. He discovered diffraction and anticipated the invention of the diffraction grating. He was one of the earliest physicists to suggest that light was wavelike in nature. He formulated a geometrical basis for a wave theory of light in his *Physico-mathesis;* this treatise attracted Isaac Newton to the study of optics. Newton deals with the diffraction problems of Grimaldi in Part III of his Opticks (1704), after having first learned of Grimaldi's diffraction from the writings of another Jesuit geometer, Honoré Fabri.

21. Paul Guldin (Swiss) b 1577 in Saint Gall d 1643 in Gratz
Reference to him in the Dictionary of Scientific Biography is found in v 1 p164, v 3 p152, v 4 p110, v 5 p 527, 588-9, v 7 p 583, v 9 p97, v 10 p301, v 13 p561, 615.
7 entries are found in Sommervogel; some examples are the following:

Problema Arithmeticum (Vienna, 1622) *de Centro Gravititatis Trium (Vienna, 1635)*

Born a Jew and named Habakuk Guldin, after his conversion he changed his name to Paul. The author D. E. Smith., in a rather hostile mood, changed Paul's name back again to Habakuk and spoke with scorn of Habakuk's humble start in life as an apprentice to a goldsmith. Paul entered the Jesuit Society as a Coadjutor Brother, and after a few years he was asked to become a Jesuit Scholastic, then was later ordained. "Guldin's rule," named in his honor, has recently been changed to "Pappus rule" by textbook authors who have been intimidated by recent careless historians.

22. Maximilian Hell (Hungarian) b 1720 in Schemnitz d 1792 in Vienna
Reference to him in the Dictionary of Scientific Biography is found in v 2 p599, v 6 p233-235, v 7 p580-1, v 10 p34, v 13 p39.
35 entries are found in Sommervogel; some examples are the following:

Ephemerides Astronomiae Anni, 1758-1806 *Elementa Mathematica (Claudipoli, 1755)*

He taught mathematics in the Jesuit college at Leutschau, Hungary (now in Czechoslovakia). Later he was made director of the astronomy observatory in Vienna. After the Suppression of the Jesuits he continued working there as director, along with other members of the Society. He fell victim to the public defamation of Jesuits then in vogue when he was accused of altering his findings during a transit of Venus. His name was not cleared until a century later when in 1883 the famous astronomer Simon Newcomb found his readings to be correct, and his scholarship above suspicion.

23. Johann Helfenzrieder (Swiss) b 1724 in Landsberg d 1803 in Reittenhaslach
26 entries are found in Sommervogel; some examples are the following:

Abhandlung von der Geodasie (Ingolstadt, 1775)
Abhandlung vom Gebrauche der Erden (Ausburg, 1794)

He taught physics at Fribourg, then geometry at Ingolstadt. He authored very accurate almanacs and published treatises on the use of telescopes, as well as on the construction of surveying apparatus. His later works include practical mechanics and the study of hydraulics.

24. Pierre Jartoux (French) b 1669 in Embrum d 1720 in Peking
Articles by him or concerning his work are found in the Philosophical Transactions of the Royal Society of London in v 28 p237-247.
7 entries are found in Sommervogel; an example is the following:
Principes pour trouver les lignes trigonométriques au moyen des séries infinies.
In his time he was considered the best Jesuit mathematician on the China mission. He presented nine remarkable theorems on infintie series, one of which concerned the direction of arcs and chords of a common circle.

25. Athanasius Kircher (German) b 1602 in Geisa d 1680 in Rome
Reference to him in the Dictionary of Scientific Biography is found in v 7 p 324-328
Articles by him or concerning his work are found in the Philosophical Transactions of the Royal Society of London in v 1 p 125-127, v 1 p 109-117, v 2 p 484-488, v 3 p 779-784, v 4 p 1093, v 4 p 967-969, v 6 p 3056-3058, v 10 p 533-542. v 12 p 1027-1029, v 13 p 208-221, v 15 p 1036-1040, v 15 p 1184-1185, v 17 p 615-617, v 17 p 865-870, v 20 p 433- 439, v 21 p 337-338, v 22 p 487 -508, v 26 p2-35.
39 entries are found in Sommervogel; some examples are the following:
Primitiae gnomonicae (Avignon, 1635) *Ars magna lucis et umbrae (Rome, 1646)*
Itinerarium extaticum (Rome, 1656) *Mundus subteraneus (Amterdam, 1665)*
Ars magna sciendi (Amsterdam, 1669) *Phonurgia nova (Kempten, 1673)*
He taught at the Roman College for many years and wrote on numerous scientific subjects, many of which were reviewed in the JSV. With his contributions on subjects such as mathematics, astronomy, harmonics, acoustics, chemistry, microscopy and medicine, he played a significant part in the early scientific revolution. In his 39 large books on the sciences, he shows learning of the past, ever open to the developments and possibilities of the future. His *Museum Kircherianum* was considered one of the best science museums in the world. Among his inventions are found the megaphone, the pantometrum for solving geometrical problems, and a counting machine. His discoveries include sea phosphorescence as well as microscopically small organisms which cause the transfer of epidemic diseases.

Kircher's works were quoted by very many scholars of the day. It was by facilitating a wide diffusion of knowledge, by stimulating thought and discussion by his vast collections of scientific information, that Kircher earned a place among the fathers of modern science and the titles of "*universal genius*" and "*master of a hundred arts.*"

26. Jacques Kresa (Moravian) b 1645 in Smrschitz d 1715 in Brunn
6 entries are found in Sommervogel; two examples are the following:
Elementos geometricos de Euclides (Cadiz, 1689)
Analysis trigonometriae sphericae (Prague, 1720)
He held "la chaire de controverse" in Prague for a number of years. In addition to his native tongue, he could converse in Latin, German, Greek, Hebrew, Italian, French, Spanish, and Portuguese.

27. Francesco Lana-Terzi (Italian) b 1631 in Brescia d in Brescia 1687
Articles by him or concerning his work are found in the Philosophical Transactions of the Royal Society of London in v 6 p3060, v 6 p2114-2116, v 7 p4068-4069, v 10 p509-512.
9 entries are found in Sommervogel; an example is the following:

Prodromo ouero saggio di alcune invenzioni nuove (Brescia, 1670)
After his studies at the Roman College, he was appointed professor of mathematics at Ferrara and Brescia. He carried out investigations on a wide range of problems in physics, and is listed as an inventor. In 1983, Belize issued a commemorative stamp of his flying ship. He earned the title "Father of Aviation" by being the first to present a scientific treatise on heavier-than-air flying machines. Although critical of Lana's flying machine, Robert Hooke wrote eleven pages concerning Lana's "Flying Chariot" in his *Philosophical Collections*, and Hooke also read long selections from Lana's *Prodromo* at the meetings of the Royal Society in 1679.

28. Antoine Laval (French) b1664 in Lyon d 1728 in Lyon
Articles by him or concerning his work are found in the Philosophical Transactions of the Royal Society of London in 25 p2241-2246.
5 entries are found in Sommervogel; an example is the following:
Voyage de la Louisian (Paris, 1728)
He was commissioned by the king to undertake astronomical expeditions. He published 54 articles in *Mémoires des Trévoux* and 11 in *Les Mémoires de l'Académie des sciences,* most of which described results of his observations of planetary motion.

29. Francis Line (English) b in London 1595 d in Liege 1675
Articles by him or concerning his work are found in the Philosophical Transactions of the Royal Society of London in v 1 p231-239, v 9 p217-219, v 9 p219, v 9 p78-83, v 10 p386-388, v 10 p499-580, v 10 p500-503, v 10 p503-504, v 11 p556-561, v 23 p1416-1418. 5 entries are found in Sommervogel; two examples are the following:
De Corporum Inseparabilitate (London, 1661) *An Explanation of the Dyall (Liege, 1673)*
He was a mathematician, physicist and scientific controversialist and was professor of mathematics at the displaced English College located in Liege. In the *Records of the English Province*, Volume VI, by Henry Foley (London: Burns & Oates, 1880), he seems also to have had other names: Butler, Hall (Thomas) and Lisle among them. Foley makes the point that many of the Jesuits at the time just disappeared and were never heard from again, so the time of death is difficult to know. He had a nephew, George Line, who was also a Jesuit. In 1669, a time when Jesuits were hanged, drawn and quartered, Line was chosen by King Charles II to construct a sundial in the garden of his Whitehall home.

30. Antoine de la Louvere (French) b 1600 in Rieux d 1664 in Toulouse
Reference to him in the Dictionary of Scientific Biography is found in v 4 p573, v 7 p583-584, v 10 p336, v 14 p749.
9 entries are found in Sommervogel; some examples are the following:
Quadratura Circuli (Toulouse, 1651) *De Cycloide Galilaei (Toulouse, 1658)*
Propositiones Geometriae (Toulouse, 1658)
Among the variations in the spelling of his name are found: de la Loubere, de la Louvere, LaLouvere, Lalouere, Loubere. He was the first geometer to study the helix. He inverted Guldin's rule to find centers of gravity; and, by the time he had the work published, he was teaching theology, which he said was much easier and more suited to his advanced age. Then, irked by an accusation of Pascal, he returned to the fray and produced a good deal more geometry concerning cycloids.

31. Paul Mako deKerck (Hungarian) b 1723 in Jasz-Apath d 1793 in Bude
24 entries are found in Sommervogel; some examples are the following:
Calculi differentialis (Trattnern, 1763) *Elementa geometrica (Bude, 1790)*

He taught geometry and physics in Vienna until the suppression of the Jesuits in1773, then he returned to Hungary. There he received ecclesiastical honors and became president of the University of Buda.

32. Charles Malapert (French) b 1580 in Mons d 1630 in Victoria
10 entries are found in Sommervogel; some examples are the following:
Faciliorum Geometriae (Douai, 1614) Euclidis Elementorum (Douai, 1620)
He taught at Pologne and Douai. His research at Douai was described in *Rosa Ursina* by Christopher Scheiner. After serving as rector of the college at Arras, he was asked by King Philip IV to teach mathematics in Madrid. He died on the way to this assignment.

33. Theodore Moretus (Belgian) b 1601 in Antwerp d 1667 in Breslau
20 entries are found in Sommervogel; some examples are the following:
Mathematici Tractatus (Prague, 1641) De luna pascali et solis motu (Wratislaviae, 1666)
He taught geometry for 14 years in Prague. His eulogy was printed in the *Memoria Sachsiana*, a medical-physics journal.

34. Pierre Nicolas (French) b 1642 in St. Flour d 1714 in Toulouse
5 entries are found in Sommervogel; some examples are the following:
De lineis logarithmeticis et Spiralibus Hyperbolicis Exercitiones (Toulouse,1696)
De Conchoidibus et Cissoidibus (Toulouse, 1697)
He taught for most of his life in Toulouse, then later became provincial. The historian Montucla mentions the impact Nicolas' studies had on the geometer Tschirnhausen in the effort to find the center of gravity of a surface of revolution.

35. Francois Noel (French) b 1651in Hestrud d 1729 in Lille
12 entries are found in Sommervogel; an example is the following:
Observationes mathematicae (Prague, 1708)
On the occasion of Robert Boyle's new pump and the newly discovered atmospheric pressure he engaged in bitter controversy with Blaise Pascal over the existence of a vacuum. He went to China in 1684, returned to France twice representing China on ceremonial occasions, then finally settled in Prague. He was also skilled in music and art.

36. Ignace G Pardies (French) b 1636 in Pau d 1673 in Bicetre
Reference to him in the Dictionary of Scientific Biography is found in v 6 p130, v 7 p583, v 10 p54, 314-315.
Articles by him or concerning his work are found in the Philosophical Transactions of the Royal Society of London in v 6 p3064-3066, v 7 p4087-4090, v 7 p4091-4093, v 7 p5012-5013, v 7 p5014- 5018, v 7 p4054, v 7 p5150-5151, v 8 p6042-6046, v 9 p219, v 26 p270-288.
16 entries are found in Sommervogel; some examples are the following:
Horologium Thaumaticum Duplex (Paris, 1662) Elemens de Géometrie (Paris, 1671)
Discours du Mouvement local (Paris, 1670)
In later life he was appointed professor of mathematics at the Collège Louis-leGrand, Paris. Pardies agreed with Huygens and Hooke in holding to the undulatory theory of light. All physicists of the day knew of his controversy with Newton over this matter, which had been reported in great detail in the Philosophical Transactions.

37. Andrea Pozzo (Italian) b 1642 in Trent d 1709 in Vienna
2 entries are found in Sommervogel; an example is the following:

Perspectiva Pictorum et Architectorum 2 vol. (Rome, 1693-1700)

He was a Jesuit Coadjutor Brother who wrote of perspective geometry applied to art. His book was one of the earliest on perspectivities and was meant to aid artists and architects. It has gone into many editions, even into this century, and has been translated from the original Latin and Italian into numerous languages such as French, German, English and Chinese. He is best known for his perspective paintings on the ceiling of St. Ignatius Church in Rome.

38. Claude Rabuel (French) b 1669 in Ain d 1728 in Lyon
1 entry is found in Sommervogel;

Commentaires sur la géometrie de Déscartes (Lyon, 1730)

He taught for 29 years in Lyons, specializing in conic sections, optics, catoptrics and optical illusions.

39. Giacomo Rho (Italian) b 1593 in Milan d 1638 in Peking
Reference to him in the Dictionary of Scientific Biography is found in v 14 p162.
28 entries are found in Sommervogel; some examples are the following:

Geometria speculativa et practica 10 vol (Wittik, 1622)
Explicatio regularum proportionum (Peking, 1630)

After being ordained by Cardinal Bellarmine he went to China in 1620. There he was commissioned to organize the imperial calendar. His Chinese name was *Lo ya kou.*

40. Vincent Riccati (Italian) b 1707 in Castel-Franco d 1775 in Italy
Reference to him in the Dictionary of Scientific Biography is found in v 11 p401-402.
28 entries are found in Sommervogel; some examples are the following:

Tomus primus opuscuorum (Bologna, 1757) Institutiones analyticae (Bologna, 1765)

He worked together with Girolamo Saladini in publishing his discovery, the hyperbolic functions - although Lambert is often incorrectly given this credit. Riccati not only introduced these new functions, but also derived the integral formulas connected with them, and then, still using geometrical methods. He then went on to derive the integral formulas for the trigonometric functions. The *Institutiones* is recognized as the first extensive treatise on integral calculus. The works of Euler and Lambert came later.

Saladini and Riccati also considered other geometrical problems, including the tractrix, the strophoid and the four-leaf rose introduced by Guido Grandi. His father Jacobi (after whom is named the *Riccati* differential equation) was one of the principal Italian mathematicians of the century, and his brother Giovanni was also a prominent mathematician.

41. Matteo Ricci (Italian) b 1552 in Macerata d 1610 in Peking
Reference to him in the Dictionary of Scientific Biography is found in v 3 p311, v 4 p457, v 7 p19, v 10 p103, v 11 p402-403, v 14 p162-4.
36 entries are found in Sommervogel; some examples are the following:

Ki ho youen pen - Geometrica Practica (*Peking, 1595* ;later reprinted in Nanking,1865)
Hoen kai tong hien tou cho - Explanation of the celestial sphere (Peking, 1607)

Against his father's wishes, who forbade any talk of religious topics around the home, Matteo Ricci entered the Jesuit Society. When his father came to bring him home from the Jesuit novitiate, he was stricken ill and took this as a sign that Matteo truly had a vocation.

Ricci arrived in China in 1583, worked there for 27 years. He was welcomed to the academies and gained many influential friendships. When the time was ripe, he opened a residence in Nanking for himself, his fellow Jesuits and his scientific instruments. Eventually he became the court mathematician in Peking. His books *Geometrica Practica* and *Trigonometrica* were translations of Clavius' works into Chinese. He made Western developments in mathematics available to the Chinese and published in 1584 and 1600 the first maps of China ever available to the West. For the first time the Chinese had an idea of the distribution of oceans and land masses. He introduced trigonometric and astronomical instruments, and translated the first six books of Euclid into Chinese.

His success was due to his personal qualities, his complete adaption to Chinese customs (choosing the attire of a Chinese scholar) and to his authoritative knowledge of the sciences. He is remembered for his Chinese works on religious and moral topics, as well as works on scientific topics such as the astrolabe, sphere, arithmetic, measure and isoperimeters. It is still possible to visit his tomb in the Peking suburbs. The Encyclopedia Britannica reports, "Probably no European name of past centuries is so well known in China as that of **Li-ma-teu** (Ricci Matteo)."

42. John Baptist Riccioli (Italian) b 1598 in Ferrara d 1671 in Bologna
Reference to him in the Dictionary of Scientific Biography is found in v 1 p483, v 3 p100 v 4 p166, v 5 p527, 542-3, v 6 p364, v 7 p326, v 8 p26, v 10 p53, v 11 p 411.
Articles by him or concerning his work are found in the Philosophical Transactions of the Royal Society of London in v 1 p 394-396, v 1 p 120-123, v 1 p 263-28, v 2 p 693-698, v 5 p 2023, v 6 p 3061-3063, v 8 p 6033-6036, v 9 p 219-222, v 11 p 611, v 13 p 244-258, v 14 p 721-726, v 16 p 314-323.
20 entries are found in Sommervogel; some examples are the following:

Almagestum Novum Astronomicum (Bologna, 1651) De Nova Cometa (Bologna, 1664) Vindiciae Kalendarii Gregorii (Bologna, 1666) Chronologiae Reformatae (Bologna, 1669)

He was professor of philosophy and theology at Parma. One of the outstanding astronomers of the century, he wrote many books on scientific as well as theological matters. His lunar map stands at the entrance to the moon exhibit at the Smithsonian Institution. It is described in detail in the Philosophical Transactions because it is the first map to name craters after scientists and prominent people instead of abstract concepts. His treatise on refraction was also reported on in the Philosophical Transactions .

43. Claude Richard (Spanish) b 1588 in Ornans d 1664 in Madrid
6 entries are found in Sommervogel; an example is the following:

Euclidis Elementorum geometricorum libri (Antwerp, 1645)

He taught geometry and Hebrew in Rome for 7 years and then requested the China mission. While on his way to China, he stopped in Lisbon, where King Philip IV, after petitioning his superiors, made him professor of mathematics at the University of Madrid, where he taught for the next forty years.

44. Girolamo Saccheri (Italian) b 1667 in San Remo d 1733 in Milan
Reference to him in the Dictionary of Scientific Biography is found in v 1 p541, v 4 p417, 451, v 6 p76, 202, v 7 p329, 330, v 8 p429, v 12 p 55-57, v 13 p510.
6 entries are found in Sommervogel; some examples are the following:

Euclides ab omni naevo vindicatus (Milan, 1733) Quaesita geometria (Milan, 1694) Logica demonstrativa (Milan, 1701)

One of his teachers was the Jesuit geometer Thomas Ceva, through whom Saccheri met Giovanni Ceva. The latter encouraged him to write his first book on coordinate geometry. He later wrote on logic and was quite concerned with the importance of definitions in mathematics. His last book, *Euclides,* prepared the way for non-Euclidean geometry. He presumed the first 28 theorems of Euclid's first book, since these did not depend on the fifth postulate, then denied the fifth postulate and attempted to find a contradiction. Eugenio Beltrami rescued this work from oblivion more than a century after it was written and showed that he deserved the title "founder of non-Euclidean geometry."

45. Gregory St. Vincent (Belgian) b 1584 in Bruges d 1667 in Gand
Reference to him in the Dictionary of Scientific Biography is found in v 5 p527, v 6 p 98, v 7 p557, v 9 p97, v 9 p311, v 10 p336, v 12 p74-76, v 13 p235, v 13 p561, v 13 p480, v 14 p148.
Articles by him or concerning his work are found in the Philosophical Transactions.
6 entries are found in Sommervogel; an example is the following:

Opus geometricum (Antwerp, 1647)

After his entrance into the Society of Jesus he studied mathematics under Christopher Clavius. St. Vincent was a brilliant mathematician and is looked upon as one of the founders of analytical geometry. He founded a famous school of mathematics at Antwerp. St. Vincent was for two years professor of geometry at Prague, where during war time his manuscript volume on geometry and statics was lost in a fire. Other papers of his were saved but carried about for ten years before they came again into his possession at his home in Ghent. They became the groundwork of his great book, the *Opus geometricum quadraturae circuli et sectionum coni, (*Antwerp, 1647). It consists of 1225 folio pages, divided into ten books.

St. Vincent deals with conics, surfaces and solids from a new point of view, employing infinitesimals in a way differing from Cavalieri. St. Vincent was probably the first to use the word *exhaurire* in a geometrical sense. From this word arose the name of "method of exhaustion," as applied to the method of Euclid and Archimedes. St. Vincent used a method of transformation of one conic into another, called *per subtendas* (by chords), which contains germs of analytic geometry. He created another special method which he called *Ductus plani in planum* and used in the study of solids. Unlike Archimedes, who kept on dividing distances only until a certain degree of smallness was reached, St. Vincent permitted the subdivisions to continue *ad infinitum* and obtained a geometric series that was infinite.

St. Vincent was the first to apply geometric series to the "Achilles" and to look upon the paradox as a question in the summation of an infinite series. Moreover, St. Vincent was the first to state the exact time and place of overtaking the tortoise. He spoke of the limit as an obstacle against further advance, similar to a rigid wall. Apparently, he was not troubled by the fact that in his theory the variable does not reach its limit. His exposition of the "Achilles" paradox was favorably received by Leibniz and by other geometers over a century later.

46. Alphonse A de Sarasa (Belgian) b 1618 in Nieveport d 1667 in Brussells
Reference to him in the Dictionary of Scientific Biography is found in v 9 p311, v 12 p25.
2 entries are found in Sommervogel; an example is the following:

Solutio problematis a R P Marino Mersenno Minimo propositi (Antwerp, 1659)

He was a pupil of Gregory St. Vincent and worked with him on showing that the area between the hyperbola and its asymptote is a logarithmic relation, thus solving the Mersenne problem of the logarithmic mean. Sarasa taught at Louvain and Antwerp. Among his other works was a book, *Ars semper gaudendi* (The art of always rejoicing) published in 1663.

47. Johann Schall von Bell (German) b 1591in Cologne d 1666 in China

29 entries are found in Sommervogel; an example is the following:
#5 Hoen tien i cho - Construction and use of the terestrial and celestial sphere
During a change of rulers he was imprisoned and condemned to a slow death, but an earthquake intervened and he was released. His *Trigonometria* and many other works were written and published in China. He constructed a double stellar hemisphere to illustrate planetary movement. He wrote 150 treatises in Chinese on the calendar. His tomb as well as those of the Jesuits Ricci and Verbiest; was restored after the Cultural Revolution and relocated on the grounds of a Communist training school. With proper authorization they can still be visited today.

48. Christopher Scheiner (German) b 1575 at Wald d 1650 Neiss
Reference to him in the Dictionary of Scientific Biography is found in v 2 p526, v 3 p528, v 5 p242, 278, 515, v 6 p361, v 7 p193, 375, v 12 p151-152, v 14 p45.
Articles by him or concerning his work are found in the Philosophical Transactions of the Royal Society of London in v 1 p143-145, v 5 p1065-1074, v 16 p535-536, v 27 p270-290.
12 entries are found in Sommervogel; some examples are the following:
Disquisitiones mathematicae de Controversis de Novitatibus astronomicis(Ingolsitadt,1614)
Refractiones Coelestes (Ingolstadt, 1617) Oculus Fundamentum opticum (Oeniponti,1619)
Rosa Ursina (Bracciani, 1626-1630) Pantographica (Rome, 1631)
He did his studies in Germany and Rome. A brilliant geometer, physicist and astronomer, he published many scientific works. He engaged Galileo in controversy, and many of his publications deal with aspects of the discussions on the systems of the universe. During his long controversy with Kepler, he adopted the pseudonym "Appelles," the mythological figure who could draw the finest line.

He discovered sunspots independently of Galileo and explained the elliptical form of the sun near the horizon as the effect of refraction. In his *Oculus* (1619) he showed that the retina is the seat of vision. His invention (1631) for magnifying curves and maps, the *pantograph,* is an early example of a geometric transformation and can still be purchased in a stationery store. He discussed the theory behind sundials (gnomonics) and their construction.

Scheiner trained young mathematicians and organized public debates on current events in astronomy, such as the heliocentric vs. the geocentric theories of the universe. In his major work, *Rosa ursina sive sol* (1630), he confirmed his findings and method and gave his measurement of the inclination of the axis of rotation of the sunspots to the plane of the ecliptic which is only off a few minutes from the true value.

49. Gaspar Schott (German) b 1608 in Koenigshofen d 1666 in Augsburg
Reference to him in the Dictionary of Scientific Biography is found in v 5 p 575, v 7 p 374-375, v 12 p 210-211, v 13 p 30.
Articles by him or concerning his work are found in the Philosophical Transactions of the Royal Society of London in v 7 p 5103-5105, v 22 p 487-508.
14 entries are found in Sommervogel; some examples are the following:
Mechanica Hydraulico-pneumatica (Wurzburg, 1657) Technica Curiosa (Wurzburg, 1680)
He was sent to Sicily to study. He worked with Kircher in Rome for three years before returning to Germany in 1655. He was appointed professor of mathematics at Augsburg. He edited a number of books by Kircher, e.g., *Pantometricum Kircherianum* and *Iter Extaticum Coeleste.* He was asked by Otto von Guericke to describe the experiment of the exhausted hemisphere, and his dramatic sketch of this experiment at Magdeburg has been copied for centuries in physics textbooks.

50. Joseph Stepling (Hungarian) b 1716 in Ratisbonne d 1778 in Prague
Reference to him in the Dictionary of Scientific Biography is found in v 7 p 490, v 12 p 39, v 13 p 39-40.
19 entries are found in Sommervogel; some examples are the following:
Exercitiones Geometrico-Analyticae (Prague, 1751)
Differentiarum minimarum (Prague, 1774)
At the age of 17 he calculated with great accuracy the 1733 lunar eclipse. Later Euler was among his long list of correspondents. He transposed Aristotelian logic into formulas, thus becoming an early precursor of modern logic. Even though he passed up a professorship in philosophy in favor of a chair in mathematics, in 1753 Empress Maria Theresa appointed him director of the faculty of philosophy at Prague as part of reform of higher education. At his death she ordered a monument to be erected in his honor in the library at the University of Prague.

51. Andre Tacquet (Belgian) b 1612 in Antwerp d 1660 in Antwerp
Reference to him in the Dictionary of Scientific Biography is found in v 1 p 164, v 1 p474, v 4 p 451, v 10 p 336, v 13 p 235, v 13 p 561.
Articles by him or concerning his work are found in the Philosophical Transactions of the Royal Society of London in v 3 p 869-876.
7 entries are found in Sommervogel; some examples are the following:
Opera Omnia Cylindricorum et Annularium (Antwerp, 1651)
Elementa Geometriae (Antwerp, 1654) *Arithmeticae Theoria et Praxis (Louvain 1656)*
He studied mathematics under Gregory St. Vincent and later taught mathematics at Louvain and Antwerp. Tacquet was a brilliant mathematician of international repute. His books were frequently reprinted, and several Italian and English editions appeared. Whiston's English edition (Cambridge, 1703) was widely used. His *Opera mathematica* was described by Henry Oldenburg as "one of the best books ever written in mathematics." His work helped pave that way for the discovery of the calculus. His use of the method of exhaustion pointed the way to the limit process later formulated by Wallis.

52. Jean Terentius (Swiss) b 1576 in Constance d 1630 in China
Reference to him in the Dictionary of Scientific Biography under the name "John Schreck" is found in v 9 p147, v 14 p162.
10 entries are found in Sommervogel; an example is the following:
Kiki tou cho - Description of mathematical instruments (Peking, 1627)
His original name was John Schreck: the Latinized form, Terentius, is more common. He was a pupil and close friend of Galileo and was admitted as the seventh member of the exclusive Academy of the Lincei; the sixth member admitted had been Galileo. The register is still extant showing the two signatures in succession. He carried Galileo's teachings and discoveries to China, and he wrote frequently to Galileo asking for assistance in correcting the Chinese calender. It was because of Terentius that Galileo's name (Chi-li-le-o) is listed with gratitude in Chinese books on astronomy. Terentius' *Trigonometria* and *De sphaerae recta constructione* were written and published in China.

53. Ferdinand Verbiest (Belgian) b 1623 in Pitthem d 1688 Peking
Reference to him in the Dictionary of Scientific Biography is found in v 14 p160-162.
Articles by him or concerning his work are found in the Philosophical Transactions of the Royal Society of London in v 16 p 39-62.
36 entries are found in Sommervogel; an example is the following:

Kouen in tou cho - Explanation of the celestial globe (Peking, 1672)

He was a geometer, astronomer and missionary to China and was a director of the Imperial Observatory in Beijing. His Chinese name was Nan Huai-Jen and he is listed as one of the 108 heroes of the popular novel Shui Hu Chuan. Having taught the Emperor geometry, science, art and literature, he became a frequent guest to the royal household. The Emperor brought him on many expeditions and entrusted him with a number of important projects of the empire. He wrote many religious works as well as a large number of astronomical and mathematical works, in the Manchu language. His funeral was a stately affair accompanied by bands, standard bearers, portraits of himself and the saints, fifty horsemen and representatives from the Emperor. His tomb in Beijing, alongside the other two giants of the China mission, Matteo Ricci and Adam Schall, was restored after the cultural revolution and can be visited today.

54. Jean B Villalpando (Spanish) b 1552 in Cordova d 1608 in Rome
Reference to him in the Dictionary of Scientific Biography is found in v 13 p29-30.
2 entries are found in Sommervogel; an example is the following:

Ezechielis explicatio (Rome, 1596-1604)

He studied geometry under the royal architect of Spain and, as a young man,was fascinated by the structure of Solomon's temple. He published works in geometry and architecture and also interpreted inscriptions both in Rome and Jerusalem along with another Jesuit, Jerome Prado; when the latter died he inherited Prado's unfinished commentary on Ezekiel. His mathematical contributions center on proportion and harmony and follow the architectural utilizations of Euclid. He produced 21 original propositions on the center of gravity and the line of direction. These can be found in the collection of Mersenne, *Synopsis mathematica* (1626). Isaac Newton used the works of Villalpando in his architectural studies.

55. Leonardo Ximenes (Italian) b 1716 in Trapani (Sicily) d 1786 in Florence
Reference to him in the Dictionary of Scientific Biography is found in v 13 p440.
51 entries are found in Sommervogel; some examples are the following:

Disertationes mechanica (Florence, 1752)
Quarta memoria idrometricae (Bologna, 1823, posthumously)

The Cathedral of Santa Maria in Florence has an inscription near the transept crediting Ximenes with making the necessary delicate measurements to align the 15th century gnomon. The meteorological observatory is named in his honor. At the time of the suppression of the Jesuits, he was able to continue his geometrical and astronomical work. He was also a highway engineer and was known for the elegance of his experimental technique in hydraulics. In his writings can be found traces of the Coriolis force (water revolving counterclockwise as it runs down a drain in the northern hemisphere), which was not defined for another century.

56. Nicolas Zucchi (Italian) b 1586 in Parma d 1670 in Rome
Reference to him in the Dictionary of Scientific Biography is found in v 14 p636-637.
17 entries are found in Sommervogel; some examples are the following:

Optica Philosphia experimentis (Rome, 1652) Machinarum omnium vires (Paris, 1646)

He taught mathematics at the Roman College and conversed often with Gaspar Schott, S.J. Laland speaks with great admiration of his invention, the reflecting telescope. He was held in such great esteem that he was sent as a papal legate to the court of the Emperor Ferdinand II, where he met Kepler; he considered this meeting one of the great moments in his life.

Appendix 2

Other Jesuit Geometers

Sommervogel lists about 18,000 publications and in his tenth volume, *Tables,* he classifies the authors according to subject matter. There are five columns of geometry, trigonometry and analytic geometry. The names not mentioned in Appendix 1 are listed here in Appendix 2. Besides these names there are fifteen more columns of names which are not listed in either Appendix because they are so numerous. These latter names have been classified as authors of books concerning applications of geometry to mechanics, hydraulics, hydrostatics, navigation, military art, astronomy and measurement. There are **487** names listed, but some of these have been listed more than once under several of the geometrical categories. The number to the left of the name is the date of publication of the major geometrical work.

1720	Albyzeta, I.	1631	Aleni, J.	1739	Alverez, G.
1758	Andre, Y.	1624	Anreiter, T.	1772	Apfalter, L.
1763	Arbosch, H.	1757	Arena, P.	1710	Attlmayr, S.
1656	Aynscom, J.	1660	Behm, G.	1751	Benvenuti, C.
1650	Berlet, J	1644	Bialkowski, N.	1758	Bohomolec, J.
1686	Bonapace, J.	1727	Borgondio, H.	1640	Bourdin, P.
1774	Cabral, E.	1735	de Campos, E.	1705	Carenna, A.
1640	Chatelard, J.	1690	Cotel, G.	1663	Courcier, P.
1578	Curtis, R.	1767	Dabutz, F.	1775	Desprotti, B.
1740	Duclos, J.	1000	Durand, J.	1781	Esseiva, P.
1633	Ferrari, A	1662	Ferroni, J.	1636	Fidati, J.
1703	Fischer, A.	1753	Fontenilles, A.	1643	Fournier, G.
1754	Frings, H.	1689	Gerbillon, J.	1754	Gleixner, F.
1704	Gooden, J.	1640	Heinz, M.	1751	Huberti, F.
1633	Inchofer, M.	1774	Jacobs, J.	1737	Janossi, N.
1747	Jerg, M.	1749	Junglingh, J.	1755	Jurewiez, S.
1707	Kirchner, M.	1755	Koerber, J.	1749	Koessler, J.
1617	Lantz, J.	1754	Lecchi, J.	1711	Leone, J.
1631	Leotaud, V	1625	Lintz, H.	1763	Luskina, E.
1698	Macrini, J.	1740	Marche, J.	1759	Marchelli, J.
1754	Mayer, C.	1801	Mickiewicz, J.	1637	Montegnana, F.
1680	Mourques, M.	1759	Nakeyanowicz, J.	1710	Nivelle, J.
1628	Pala, S.	1770	Palmieri, H.	1615	Pennequin, P.
1781	Perez, F.	1766	Perouse, J.	1749	Pezenas, E.
1750	Pfeffer, H.	1782	Pickel, I.	1772	Poezobut, M.
1793	Rainis, J.	1771	Riedthaler, M.	1767	Rostan, A.
1726	Rouille, P.	1765	Sanvitale, F.	1766	Saracinelli, A.
1776	Schauer, A.	1770	Scherffer, C.	1686	Solski, S.
1732	Spedalieri, M.	1776	Spengler, J.	1630	Stafford, I.
1668	Streitt, T.	1694	Sxekeli, F.	1773	Tessaneck, J.
1711	Thullner, J.	1730	Tosch, C.	1775	Trentel, F.
1692	Tylkowski, A.	1707	Vorster, G.	1689	Waibl, A.
1754	Walcher, J.	1738	Weilhamer, A.	1774	Wydra, S.
1770	Zinner, I.	1671	Zaragosa, J.	1769	Zebrowski, T.
1790	Zeiller, J.	1769	Zeno, F.	1769	Zeplichal, A.

Appendix 3 Chronology

In these four columns are shown corresponding chronologies with important events in world history, mathematical history, Jesuit history and in the lives of the 56 Jesuit geometers. Three year intervals **(3yr)** are indicated between the years 1564 and 1776. Inevitably dates for the events in all four columns do not coincide exactly, so that the dates in the Jesuit columns are only approximate.

Mathematics History	World History		Jesuit History	Jesuit Geometers
1545 Cardan: Ars Magna	1547 d Henry VIII	(3yr)	Jesuits founded (1540)	b Clavius, Ricci (1538)
- - - -	- - - -		- - - -	- - - -
1564 b Galileo	1564 b Shakespeare; C Trent	1564	Jesuits in Florida	b Grienberger
1569 Mercator: *Cosmographia*	1569 40,000 die in Lisbon	67	Douai College for exiled English Jesuits	b d'Aguilon
1572 Bombelli: *Algebra*	1571 Battle of Lepanto	70	Univ Pont-a-Mousson founded by S.J.	b Scheiner
1571 b Kepler	1573 b Michelangelo	73	Start of Counter Reformation	Clavius: *In sphaeram de Sacrobosco*
1576 d Girolamo Cardan	1577 b Peter Paul Rubens	76	5,000 Jesuits: 140 Jesuit colleges	b Guldin
1579 Viete: *Canon mathematicus*	1580 7th French war Religion	79	Edmund Campion's trial	b Malapert
1581 isochronous property of pendula	1584 assass. of William Orange	82	beginning of Jesuit China Mission	b Bettini
1585 Stevin: *La disme*	1588 b Marin Mersenne	85	English martyrs	b G. St. Vincent, Zucchi
1588 b Marin Mersenne	1588 defeat of Spanish Armada	88	Bellarmine: *de Controversiis*	b Schall von Bell, Richard
1590 Galileo: *de Motu*	1590 Vatican Library opens	91	Jose Acosta, S.J.: *History of Indians*	b Rho, Line
1595 Pitiscus: *Trigonometria*	1594 d John of the Cross	94	d. Peter Canisius	b de la Faille
1596 Kepler: *de Admirabili*	1598 Edict Nantes	97	Ratio Studiorum	b de la Louvere
1601 d Tycho Brahe	1600 Kircher's magic lantern	1600	Robert Southwell hanged	b Moretus, Kircher
1603 d Viete	1603 d Elizabeth I	03	Beginning of Paraguay Reductions (1607)	b de Billy, Ciermans
1606 Galileo's telescope	1606 Guy Fawkes sentenced	06	Henry IV recalls Jesuits back to France	b Fabri, Schott, d Villalpando
1609 Kepler: *Astronomia nova*	1607 Galileo's telescope	09	Jesuits in Canada	b Tacquet, Grimaldi
1614 Napier's logarithms	1614 d Shakespeare,Cervantes	12	Suarez: *Defensio Fidei*	d Clavius, Ricci
1613 Pitiscus' table of sines	1615 Galileo faces Inquisition	15	Belgian School of Mathematics started	b Casati, de Sarasa
1620 Burgi's logarithms	1618 beginning of 30-Year War	18	13,000 Jesuits in 32 Provinces	b de Chales
1623 b Blaise Pascal	1620 Pilgrims land	21	d Robert Bellarmine	b Verbiest
1625 b Jean Cassini	1626 d F Bacon, W Snell	24	Ignatius and Xavier canonized	Scheiner: *Rosa ursina*
1629 Fermat's method of max/min	1627 b Robert Boyle	27	Peter Claver, S.J., mission in Catagena	b de Gottignies
1631 Harriot: *Artis analyticae praxis*	1628 Richelieu attacks Huguenots	1630	Giulio Alenio, S.J.:Chinese *Life of Christ*	b Lana-Terzi
1635 Cavalieri:*Geometria indivisibilibus*	1635 b Robert Hooke	33	*Arc* and *Dove* arrive in Maryland	Ciermans: *Repetitio menstrua*
1637 Descartes: *Discours de la method*	1636 Harvard College	36	Start of *Jesuit Relations*	b Pardies
1639 Desargues: *Bruillon projet*	1637 France enters 30-Year War	39	d John Francis Regis, S.J.	b Bonfa
1642 b Newton; d Galileo	1643 Accession of Louis XIV	42	Antonio Escobar, S.J.: *Theologia moralis*	b Nicolas, Pozzo
1646 b Leibniz	1644 Torricelli's barometer	45	Bolandists' revised *Acta Sanctorum*	b de Fontaney
1647 d Cavalieri and Torricelli	1648 end of 30-Year War	48	North American martyrs	b Kresa, Ceva
1651 b René Descartes	1651 Von Guericke's pump	51	150,000 Chinese converts	b Noel
1655 Wallis: *Arithmetica infinitorum*	1654 Magdeburg hemisphere exper.	54	Simon Le Moyne, S.J. Onondagas mission	Tacquet: *Elementa Geometriae*
1658 Huygens' cycloidal pendulum clock	1660 English monarchy restored	57	d Andrew Bobola, S.J.	b Bouvet

Mathematics History	World History		Jesuit History	Jesuit Geometers
1661 d Gerard Desargues	1662 Royal Society founded	1660	d Robert de Nobili, S.J.	Fabri: *Opusculum geometricum*
1667 b Abraham de Moivre	1665 *Journal des Savants*	63	Trappists founded	b Laval
1667 Gregory: *Geometriae universalis*	1666 Académie des Sciences	66	Ottawa mission begins	b Saccheri
1668 Mercator: *Logarithmotechnia*	1668 Hooke: on earthquakes	69	Construction of Sant' Andrea al Quirinale	b Jartoux
1670 Barrow: *Lectiones geometriae*	1671 Leibniz' calculator	72	Marquette's exploration of Mississippi	b Rabuel
1673 Huygens: *Horologium Oscillatorum*	1674 Milton's *Paradise Lost*	75	K Louis' confessor: Francois de la Chaise	Zucchi: reflecting telescope
1675 b Giles Roberval	1677 d Henry Oldenburg	78	Painting of St. Ignatius Church in Rome	Kircher: *Ars magna sciendi*
1678 Ceva's theorem	1682 Acta eruditorum found	81	d Claude La Colombiere, S.J.	Schott: *Technica curiosa*
1684 Leibniz' first paper on calculus	1683 Siege of Vienna	84	"Mathematiciéns Royal" sent to China	d Lana-Terzi
1687 Newton: *Principia*	1685 Edict of Nantes revoked	87	Alexendre de Rhodes: Indochina mission	b Castel
1690 Rolle: *Traite d'algebre*	1690 Battle of Boyne	1690	119 disguised Jesuits teaching in England	Ceva: *de Cycloide*
1692 d Voltaire	1692 MacDonnells at Glencoe	93	d John deBritto	b Jartoux
1696 Brachistochrone, L'Hospital's rule	1694 b Voltaire	96	Japanese martyrs	Pozzo: *Perspectiva*
1698 b Colin Maclaurin	1698 Ozanam rejects 4th dimension	99	Decision against the Chinese Rites	b Beraud
1704 b Gabriel Cramer	1701 Journal de Trévoux	02	Beginning of *Journal de Trévoux*	Bonfa: *Binocle geometrique*
1706 Use of π by William Jones	1703 Peter G defeats Charles VII	05	French Jesuits: *Dictionnaire de Trévoux*	Noel: *Observationes mathematique*
1707 b Leonard Euler	1706 b Ben Franklin	08	Jesuits operate 612 colleges	b Riccati
1713 Cotes: revises Newton's *Principia*	1711 b Hume	11	d Eusebio Kino, S.J.	b Boscovich
1715 Taylor: *Methoda incrementorum*	1712 b Frederick the Great	14	Philippines' publications of Pavel Klein	b Ximenes
1718 DeMoivre: Doctrine of Chance	1712 Treaty of Utrecht	17	Decree banishing Jesuits from China	b Amiot,Stepling
1718 b Maria Gaetana Agnesi	1718 New Orleans founded	1720	Expulsion of Jesuits from Russia	b Hell
1722 Cotes: *Harmonia mensurarum*	1721 Bach: Brandenburgs	23	d Anthony Baldinucci, S.J.	b Mako de Kerck
1727 d Isaac Newton	1724 b Emmanuel Kant	26	7,765 men in the German Assistancy	Kresa: *Analysis trigonometriae*
1728 b Johann Lambert	1729 b Catherine the Great	29	General Congregation 16 on modern science	b Abad, Alegre
1730 Stirling's formula b Lalande	1730 Pope: *Essay on man*	32	Malabar Rites controversy	Castel: *Plan d'une Mathématique*
1733 Saccheri: *Euclid Vindicated*	1736 b Joseph LaGrange	35	Jesuits in Syria	Saccheri: *Euclides ab omni naevo*
1738 Dan Bernoulli:*Hydrodynamica*	1740 Accession of Frederick the Great	38	Gottfried Laimbeckhoven, S.J. in Hukwang	Boscovich: *Trigonometriae sphaer.*
1742 Goldbach's conjecture	1742 Centigrade thermometer	41	57 Christian communities in Paraguay	Regis' *Jesuit map of China*
1742 Maclaurin: *Treatise of Fluxions*	1744 Louis XV declares war on Austria	44	2,300 Jesuits working in Spanish America	Hell: *Elementa mathematica*
1743 D'Albembert: *Traité de dynamique*	1746 Princeton College founded	47	Jesuits run 176 seminaries, 15 universities	Stepling: *Exercitiones geometrico*
1748 Euler:*Introductio*;Agnesi:*Istituzioni*	1751 Diderot's *Encyclopédie*	750	Edict ordering Paraguay Reductions closed	Ximenes: *Disertationes mechanica*
1750 Cramer's rule; Fagnano's ellipse	1752 Franklin's kite	53	200,000 students in 721 Jesuit colleges	Stepling: *Exercitationes Geometrico*
1758 Montucla:*Histoire mathématiques*	1755 Moscow Univ founded	56	Expulsion of Jesuits from Portugal	Riccati: *Opusculorum*
1761 Lambert: π is irrational	1758 Pombal expels Jesuits	59	Copernicus removed from Index (Boscovich)	Boscovich: *Philosophiae naturalis*
1765 d Clairaut	1760 Canada under British rule	62	Society dissolved in France	d Castel
1765 Euler's solution Pell's equation	1764 Brown Univ founded	65	D'Alembert's *Destruction des Jésuites*	Mako: *Calculi differentialis*
1768 b Fourier	1767 Watt's engine	68	End of the Paraguay Reductions	Riccati: *Institutiones analyticae*
1770 Hyperbolic trigonometry	1770 Boston massacre	71	Expulsion of Jesuits from Spain	Alegre: *Elementorum geometricae*
1772 Euler: *Mechanices*	1774 Discovery of oxygen	774	Suppression of the Society (1773)	d Riccati
- - - -	- - - -		- - - -	- - - -
1777 b Carl Gauss	1776 Declaration of Independence	77	Jesuit Society in Russia: Georgetown U	d Boscovich

Some other

Jesuit Geometers

and their

Geometry

Saccheri

Saint Vincent

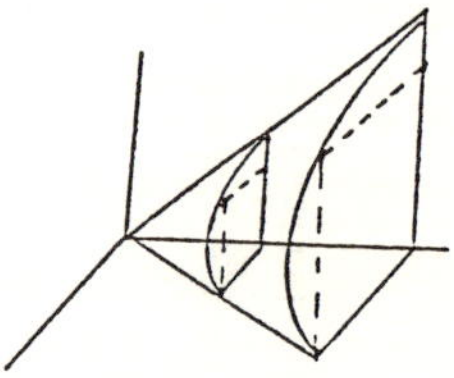

Clavius

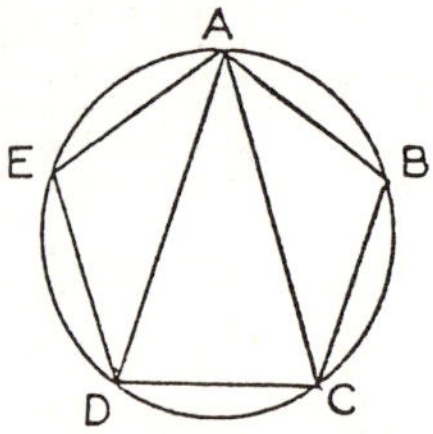

de la Louvere

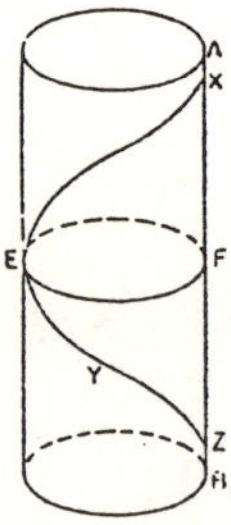

de Chales

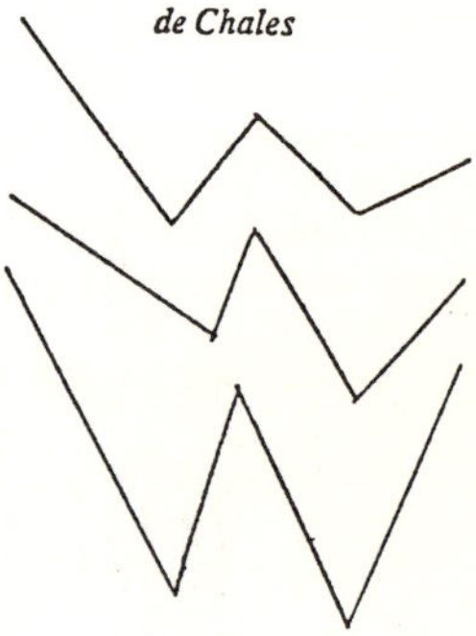

Ceva

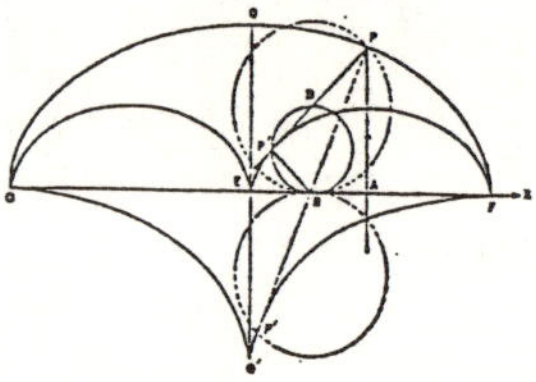

Pardies

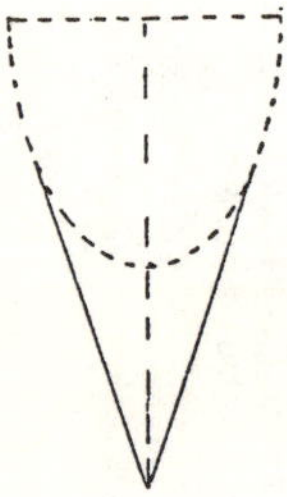

Tacquet

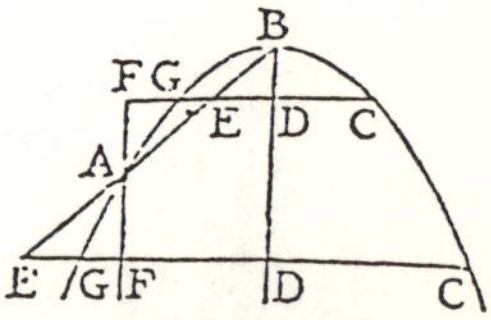

Kircher

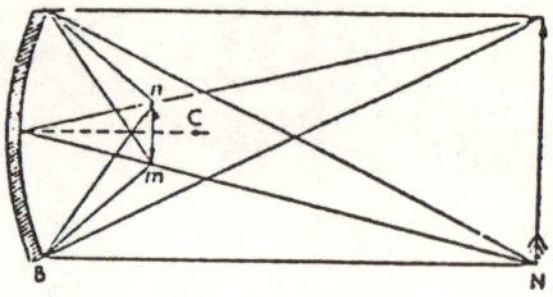

Index